MOVING
BEYOND
QUADRANT A:
DEVELOPING RIGOR, RELEVANCE, AND
LEARNER ENGAGEMENT IN YOUR CLASSROOM

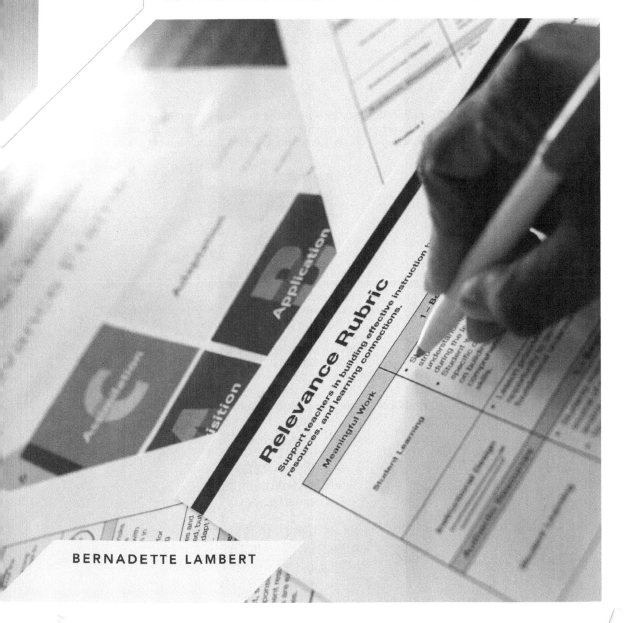

BERNADETTE LAMBERT

Copyright © 2016 by International Center for Leadership in Education, Inc.
All rights reserved.
Published by International Center for Leadership in Education, Inc.
Printed in the U.S.A.

ISBN-13: 978-1-328-01232-6
ISBN-10: 1-328-01232-8

International Center for Leadership in Education, Inc.
1587 Route 146
Rexford, New York 12148
(518) 399-2776
fax (518) 399-7607
www.LeaderEd.com
info@LeaderEd.com

1 2 3 4 5   0014   20 19 18 17 16
4510002258   ABCDE

Dedication

For teachers
—yesterday, today, and tomorrow—
who stoke curiosity,
stretch imagination,
and stress agency.

Contents

Acknowledgments

I am both humbled and proud to work with such an exceptional team of thinkers and leaders. Together, we moved beyond Quad A to create an amazing resource for teachers.

Thank you, Kelly Griego. Your brilliance and creativity breathed life into this body of work. Throughout the process, you have been my collaborator, editor, friend, and teacher.

Thank you, Dr. Linda Lucey, for choosing me to take this journey. With your guidance and support, I continue to grow as an educator and as a writer.

Thank you, Kris Ross, for your editing savvy. Your positive attitude encouraged me, and your attention to detail reassured me.

Thank you, fellow consultants who read, reviewed, and offered feedback.

Thank you, Dr. Bill Daggett for inviting me on this ICLE adventure so many years ago.

Foreword

Rigor and relevance is a concept that has been embraced by many in the American K–12 education system. As a Senior Fellow for the International Center for Leadership in Education, Bernadette Lambert has partnered with schools and districts across the nation, meeting them where they are and moving them to the next level of learning.

I have worked with the nation's most rapidly improving schools for more than two decades, and have seen up close how moving instruction and learning from Quadrant A—low rigor, low relevance—to Quadrant D—high rigor, high relevance—is the key to success. Knowing that we must do this and knowing *how* to do this requires a second-nature understanding of what rigor and relevance are, in addition to what true learner engagement looks like. Bernadette has made it her mission to help you achieve that understanding once and for all. *Moving Beyond Quadrant A: Developing Rigor, Relevance, and Learner Engagement in Your Classroom* is a deep dive into the Rigor/Relevance Framework®, coupled with strategies and tactics to bring rigor, relevance, and learner engagement to life in your own classroom.

In Part One, Bernadette begins with some supportive, inspiring "straight talk," as she calls it, about the realities of our education world. Yes, there are challenges, but we educators still have control of our classrooms. Let's focus on what we can change. We have agency and the power to make choices that have a direct impact on those in front of us: our students. We can do this by focusing on increasing rigor, extending relevance, and encouraging engagement. Bernadette walks you through these concepts of rigor, relevance, and engagement in a way that will allow you to see them, know them, and embrace them in a new light. Have you ever considered rigor as driven by curiosity? Or relevance as driven by imagination? And engagement as a function of agency? By thinking about these concepts in a new way yet in familiar language, applying them in your classroom and explaining them to your students will become that much easier.

In Part Two, Bernadette provides strategies that align to the nine indicators of the Rigor, Relevance, and Engagement rubrics, which are tools to help you methodically implement and account for each in your classroom. These strategies frame your thinking as you design instruction and guide your students through learning opportunities and discussion that move them beyond Quad A. In Part Three, you will find 33 tactics, tools, and techniques that support the strategies. Consider this your toolbox to advance your goal of getting closer and closer to Quad D—until it becomes habit.

Those who read this book will emerge with a clear grasp on how to make rigor, relevance, and engagement the underpinnings of everything that happens in the classroom—and why you must. Those who read this book will, I think, become students of rigor and relevance themselves, and, as Bernadette says, adopt a Quad D attitude that will guide and enhance instruction for years to come.

This is a book every K–12 educator should read. As the creator of the Rigor/Relevance Framework, I am grateful to Bernadette for this tremendous contribution to our commitment to assist all educators, especially teachers, to move rigor, relevance, and engagement from concept to reality in their classroom.

Thank you, Bernadette.

Bill Daggett, Ed.D.
Founder and Chairman
International Center for Leadership in Education

Introduction

When Dr. Bill Daggett asked me to write a book explaining how to bring rigor, relevance, and engagement to life in the classroom, I will confess my immediate reaction: I was struck with a bit of fear. My concern was not about what I'd put in the book, but what I'd leave out. How could a complete and lasting list of instructional tools, techniques, and tactics ever fit in one book—particularly those that are applicable to teachers of all subjects and grade levels?

Like any good student of rigor and relevance, like anyone with a Quad D attitude, I talked myself down and decided to see this opportunity for what it was: The incredible chance to do more than provide instructional tactics. An opportunity to help educators, finally, get unstuck from the tactical muck, and instead gain a 360-degree view—see the forest for the trees, if you will. An opportunity to help educators truly comprehend rigor, relevance, and engagement so they can embody these concepts, model them, and master them. An opportunity to help teachers feel in control of their classrooms!

While this book does include dozens of instructional tactics, they are not the only point. I hammer this home throughout the book; any tactic is only as good as the strategy it serves. And any strategy is only as useful as its goal is worthy and intentional. Instructional tactics evolve, trend, change with technology, and fall in and out of favor; if they are the sole focus of an instructional book, that book will become outdated—and fast. For this book to serve educators over the long term, it needs to help you grasp concepts so that you can begin to create your own tactics or learn how to spot those that advance your larger strategic goals. That's teaching a person how to fish, rather than just handing him or her dinner. Tactics are important; understanding their larger strategic context is what will fundamentally change you and your classroom.

This is the hope of this book, that it will leave you *knowing* the Rigor/Relevance Framework®. It is my hope that you, dear reader, will see how rigor, relevance, and engagement come together as a strategic goal for your classroom; that you will feel confident navigating and using the Rigor, Relevance, and Learner Engagement Rubrics as a guide to intentional instructional design. *To get this view, I encourage you to read the book from start to finish.*

I begin by explaining rigor, relevance, and engagement in language that you will find familiar and, I hope, fun and interesting. And I mean that! This is no dry academic text. I pepper this book with history, anecdotes, ideas, and cultural figures so that we both can enjoy this process. I use a mix of research and my own experience—from my ten years in the classroom and now more than a decade as a literacy strategist and coach—to show you, not just tell you, what rigor, relevance, and learner engagement look like in the classroom. Then I move into strategies and tactics so you can bring these concepts to your own classroom. They will only make sense to you if you've read Part One of the book first. Doing so is what one with a Quad D attitude would do anyhow.

Share what you learn here with your students. If they are to engage in their learning, they must be invited into it. Be transparent with why you're increasing rigor and extending relevance; this is the only way to make them active agents of their learning. Share what you learn here with your colleagues and peers. Exchange ideas, strategies, and tactics. Seek opportunities to collaborate with them and support each other as we all strive to bring intentional instructional design to our classrooms. And have some fun.

Fear of failure is a natural part of any lofty goal we set out to reach. Yet I decided to embrace a Quad D attitude and persevere with the challenge set before me. As you read this book, I encourage you to do the same. As someone who strives always to apply rigor and relevance in her lifelong learning, as someone who aims to be an active agent in her own life, I am truly flattered to have been asked to write this book, fears and all. I'm delighted you're joining me.

Bernadette Lambert

Part One

Rigor, Relevance, and Learner Engagement

Rigor, Relevance, and Engagement Personified

In 1956, Simpson College dedicated the Carver Science Center in honor of one of its most esteemed alumni: George Washington Carver. At the dedication, Nobel Prize winner Ralph Bunche described Carver as "the least imposing celebrity the world has ever known" (Vella, 2015). At the time of his death in 1943, Carver called Presidents Theodore Roosevelt, Calvin Coolidge, and Franklin Delano Roosevelt his friends. Well-known titans of industry and science, including Harvey Firestone, Henry Ford, Thomas Edison, and John Burroughs, were among his confidantes. Over the course of his career as an agricultural scientist and inventor, Carver fielded multiple requests from governments in countries near and far to solve horticultural puzzles (Vella, 2015). He was invited to speak before Congress, won academic awards and medals of honor, and was asked to join elite arts and letters societies. By all accounts, Carver had international fame. Nonetheless, he was said to be a quiet, humble, modest man, dedicated to his curiosity, and not without a sense of humor (Vella, 2015).

Carver was born a slave in 1864 in Missouri. His father died before he was born, and his mother died when he was just an infant. As a baby, he was kidnapped by Confederate raiders, held for ransom, and traded back to his original owners—Moses and Susan Carver, who became legal guardians to him and his brother James. Susan insisted that the young children, who were freed after the Civil War, learn to read and get a formal education. Due to the dearth of nearby schools that would accept African-American students, Carver was forced to piece together an education at various, often distant schools, one of which was 10 miles from the Carver farm—a commute that Carver walked each day. When formal education was inaccessible to these young boys, Susan attempted to compensate. She recognized Carver's strong intellect and fascination with plant life. When he would help Susan with kitchen and gardening chores, she let him experiment with natural herbicides, pesticides, antifungals, and soil conditioners. While still just a child, Carver became known to local farmers as "the plant doctor," and was sought after for agricultural tips.

Carver went on to complete high school, earning his tuition by baking in a hotel kitchen. He was known to tinker with recipes and create his own. He applied to college, was accepted, and was offered a full scholarship, only to have it all rescinded when the school discovered he was African American. Carver remained determined and resilient. Eventually, he enrolled as the first African-American student at Simpson College in Iowa, and then later studied botany at Iowa State Agricultural School, where he was the first African American to graduate with a bachelor of science. As a student, he produced research so groundbreaking that school staff offered him a job running the Iowa State Experimental Station. During his tenure, he made several discoveries that elevated him to the status of a pre-eminent agricultural scientist.

Booker T. Washington, founder of Tuskegee Institute in Alabama, got word of Carver's contributions to science. In 1896, Washington sent Carver a letter that read: "I cannot offer you money, position, or fame. The first two you have. The last from the position you now occupy you will no doubt achieve. These things I now ask you to give up. I offer you in their place: work—hard work, the task of bringing people from degradation, poverty, and waste to full manhood. Your department exists only on paper and your laboratory will have to be in your head"

(Bagley, 2013). Without pause, Carver rose to the challenge, finding great honor in the prospect of helping African-American farmers in the rural South lift themselves from poverty.

What followed was a life filled with stories upon stories about a man who wanted to learn about everything. He was an inventor, a trailblazer, an advocate. His influence on science was profound and is still renowned today. His impact on the farmers he worked with was tangible, as he empowered them with knowledge that increased their skills and enabled their economic freedom. Carver was born into a world where all the cards were stacked against him. He was categorically not welcome in most areas of society, yet this never seemed to deter him. With his steadfast persistence to pursue his passions, he knocked down wall after wall, making it a little bit easier for those who followed. I could write a book on all that this man achieved in his life against the odds. Many have. But for our purposes here, I will share a story about his work with newly freed African-American farmers.

Cotton was the predominant crop on southern farms; however, it depleted the soil, resulting in smaller and smaller harvests—a fact that was impeding the success of sharecroppers as they attempted to find their footing in post-Reconstruction America. Carver knew that these farmers did not have the means to come to him to learn. So he invented what he called the Jesup Wagon, a horse-drawn, mobile chemistry lab that Carver took to the farmers. He introduced them to the idea of crop rotation to replenish soil nutrients. His favorite crop for this purpose was peanuts; through experimentation, Carver discovered that peanuts have nitrogen-fixing properties that improved cotton output. By folding this knowledge into their farming, his "students" saw incredible cotton growth and were thrilled (Bagley, 2013). However, they were less thrilled with the surplus of peanuts that came with it, which, in the South, generated little demand or return.

Carver heard his students' complaints, and his response is something that I've never forgotten. He retired to his laboratory for, it is said, only one week and emerged with a collection of products he dreamed up and made from peanuts. He then introduced and marketed these products by way of a bulletin distributed to the local community. Out of seeming thin air, Carver created a market and a demand for peanut products and promoted peanuts as a cash crop that sharecroppers could sell to their benefit (Merritt, 1929). To this day, this move is said to have saved the agricultural economy of the rural South. All told, Carver came up with about three hundred uses for peanuts in goods such as insulation paper, flour, paste, soap, shaving cream, body lotion, and even a few medicinal products (Bagley, 2013).

I share this story not to suggest that each of our students must go on to make their marks in the annals of history. That's unrealistic. I share it simply because this story—and this man—is one that has always struck me as capturing the full essence of rigor, relevance, and engagement. An invitation to work hard despite few resources or assistance? Carver was undaunted. He accepted the risk with confidence. The challenge to help educate farmers who had no means to gain an education? No problem, Carver took it upon himself to find a way to take the education to them. An unintended consequence of a peanut surplus that was creating problems for the very farmers he was trying to help? Discouraged by this feedback he was not. Just give the man one week. Carver's solution to the peanut problem was so creative, so original, and was made possible by his ability to connect the dots of his vast and varied knowledge.

In this story, we see Carver apply the fruits of his enormous curiosity. We see him exercise imagination to discover solutions to problems he did and did not expect. And we see him use his agency— his voice, his humble power, his wherewithal—to make the necessary decisions to address setbacks, work productively and respectfully with his students, and achieve success with them. If this is not rigor, relevance, and engagement in action, I do not know what is. If this man did not embody a Quad D attitude, then I do not know who does.

Chapter One

Nurturing a Quad D Attitude

The Rigor/Relevance Framework®

The entirety of this book is devoted to explaining, capturing, and unpacking what the Rigor/Relevance Framework is and how to use the Rigor, Relevance, and Engagement Rubrics to elevate and evaluate instruction and learning in your classroom. Its primary aim is to show you what rigor, relevance, and engagement look like in the classroom and how to achieve it in yours. And my goal is to do this in language that is simple, relatable, familiar, approachable, and, I hope, even a little fun. But first we need to get a little technical to introduce the Framework and rubrics.

The Rigor/Relevance Framework was constructed in 1991 by Dr. Bill Daggett, Founder and Chairman of the International Center for Leadership in Education (ICLE). It was born of a desire to help provide educators a way to think about, plan, and assess levels of complex thinking and applicability to the real world. The Framework begins with the six levels of the Revised Bloom's Knowledge Taxonomy (Anderson & Krathwohl, 2001), which are arranged vertically going upward on the rigor axis, or the thinking continuum. Those levels—Remembering, Understanding, Applying, Analyzing, Evaluating, and Creating— capture the increasing intellectual power of a student's cognitive effort as thinking and knowledge depth move up the rigor axis (Anderson & Krathwohl, 2001). At the low end of the continuum, the student recalls knowledge merely to recall knowledge. At the high end, the student can take multiple bits of knowledge and combine them creatively and logically.

A: Teacher Works

B: Student Works

C: Student Thinks

D: Student Works & Thinks

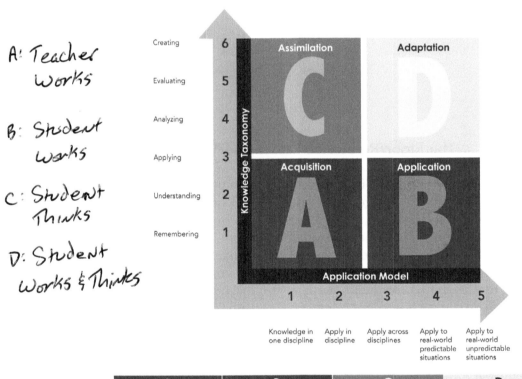

Rigor/Relevance Framework®

A	B	C	D
Students gather and store bits of knowledge and information. Students are primarily expected to remember or understand this knowledge.	Students use acquired knowledge to solve problems, design solutions, and complete work. The highest level of application is to apply knowledge to new and unpredictable situations.	Students extend and refine their acquired knowledge to be able to use that knowledge automatically and routinely to analyze and solve problems and create solutions.	Students think in complex ways and can apply their knowledge and skills. Even when confronted with perplexing unknowns, students can create solutions and take action that further develops their skills and knowledge.

Dr. Daggett created the Application Model to convey the increasingly complex ways students can apply the knowledge they learn to scenarios outside of the classroom. The five points on the horizontal relevance axis, also called the action continuum, represent the actions one can take with knowledge. At the low end of the continuum, knowledge is applied to one discipline. At the high end, it can be applied to real-world scenarios, both predictable and unpredictable.

I have found it helpful to think of rigor—which moves up and down—as the depth of learning, and relevance—which moves side to side—as the breadth of learning. Rigor is something we want to raise, and relevance is something we want to extend. Anyone who has heard Dr. Daggett speak knows his common refrain, "Relevance makes rigor possible." It's a simple idea that can lead to transformative results. By finding ways to make a learning task relevant to a student, by differentiating it just enough to fit his or her interests, that student's capacity for rigor naturally expands. If you know your math student loves tennis, then you can extend relevance to meet her interests by crafting a word problem about calculating the rate at which a tennis ball travels when it goes X distance for Y amount of time. Since this topic is of personal interest to her, willingness to think rigorously will rise. *Relevance makes rigor possible.*

The overlay of the Application Model on the Knowledge Taxonomy yields four quadrants. Each quadrant reveals the degree to which both rigor and relevance are utilized; i.e., Quad A, acquisition; Quad B, application, Quad C, assimilation; Quad D, adaptation. The quadrants allow educators and learners to determine how complex their thinking and how relevant their use of it will be or was in a given task or conversation. If instruction or learning is in Quad A, both rigor and relevance are low. In Quad B, action is high, but is taken with low rigor thinking. In Quad C, thinking is complex and cognitive effort is rigorous, but application and relevance to the real world is low. In Quad D, we reach a sort of rigor and relevance nirvana, where students can flexibly apply broad knowledge to various real-world scenarios, predictable and unpredictable, and demonstrate the capacity to generate new ideas from existing information.

The Rigor, Relevance, and Engagement Rubrics

Getting to Quad D is challenging. Yet it is doable with clear goal setting, strategic planning, and a broad suite of tools to support intentional instructional design. It also takes maintenance. ICLE created the Rigor, Relevance, and Engagement Rubrics as, first and foremost, an instructional design and planning tool for teachers. The rubrics are meant to help educators plan, evaluate, and monitor the efficacy of their deliberate instructional design and the instruction's capacity to achieve the student learning results they intended. They are a tool to help teachers be proactive, not reactive, in their instruction, while also providing a framework to think about where instruction is falling short on realizing desired outcomes and how improvements can be made.

The inclusion of engagement provides a framework for sustaining rigor and relevance over the long term by keeping students motivated and accountable. Engagement in the classroom also prepares students for life in college, where instruction becomes less nurturing, and life in careers, where it's incumbent upon the individual to excel in and maintain his or her job. Engagement extends responsibility for learning to each student.

There are nine indicators on the rubrics: three for each of the three categories. In the Rigor category, the indicators are High-Level Questioning, Academic Discussion, and Thoughtful Work. In the Relevance category, the indicators are Meaningful Work, Authentic Resources, and Learning Connections. Finally, in the Engagement category, the indicators are Active Participation, Learning Environment, and Formative Processes and Tools.

Each indicator is split into a Student Learning section and an Instructional Design section. From there, each indicator is then divided into four levels of aptitude and evidence of use in the classroom—Beginning, Emerging, Developed, and Well Developed—with descriptive text in each. The rubric can help educators pinpoint where on the aptitude spectrum their instructional design sits and, thus, where and how they can improve. The rubrics also describe the extent to which there is evidence that intended student learning outcomes are being achieved across indicators. By observing student behavior in the classroom, the teacher can refer back to the rubrics to determine where instructional design might be failing to elicit the desired learning outcome. (The full rubrics can be found at www.leadered.com/RRERubrics.)

High-Level Questioning	1—Beginning	2—Emerging	3—Developed	4—Well Developed
Student Learning	• Students respond to questions that mainly focus on basic recall and retell. • Few students ask questions, and most questions asked focus on basic recall or retelling of content.	• Students respond to questions that demonstrate a comprehension of content. • Students have opportunities to ask questions during the lesson and most questions focus on comparing and contrasting information.	• Students fully explain and justify their thinking when responding to questions that demonstrate different levels of thinking, including questions that require analysis, synthesis, and evaluation of information. • During the lesson, students generate questions about content that demonstrate rigorous independent thinking.	• Students actively engage in developing rigorous questions to challenge the thinking of their peers. • Students are able to respond to rigorous questions generated by peers with little guidance from the teacher.
Instructional Design	• Lesson mainly includes questions at the recall and retell level, and/or not all students are required to respond to each question.	• Lesson includes questions at a range of levels, but not all students are required to respond to each question.	• Lesson uses questioning to carefully support students in moving to higher levels of thinking, ensuring that all students have an opportunity to respond.	• Lesson is designed to inspire all students to engage in high-level questioning around the learning task with their teachers and peers.

Any teacher with the Framework and the rubrics in hand is light years ahead of those who simply show up in the classroom and hope that students also show up prepared. To acknowledge that instruction must be goal-oriented, strategic, intentional, and regularly monitored and evaluated for impact and efficacy is half the battle. In fact, it's the most important step to take.

I'd like to consider the more technical portion of this presentation over. Let's get to the fun part: learning how to intentionally create powerful rigorous, relevant, and engaging classrooms that our students will look forward to visiting each day and remember for years to come.

First, some straight talk.

Let's Be Frank. Let's Be Realistic. Let's Be Positive.

If we are going to have any realistic hope of improving our instructional outcomes and the futures of our students, then we must speak candidly. We are at a critical point in education in our country. We all know it. We're amid a confluence of challenging circumstances. Our student population grows only more diverse and in an increasing number of ways. Many students do not speak English as a first language, which presents obvious comprehension challenges. There's much discussion about how our entire system is outdated and at odds with its mandate to prepare students for the future. Many believe that our instructional practices remain stuck in twentieth-century thinking, which emphasizes routine tasks over the complicated and cross-disciplinary tasks that twenty-first-century jobs require. Policy seems to change with the wind. We educators are repeatedly scrambling to learn and adopt the latest policy and adapt our instruction to meet standards. All the while, we are taking our eyes off the thing that matters most, the reason we got into this line of work to begin with: the students.

It's no wonder so many of us in education feel exhausted, overwhelmed, and burnt out. How could one not with all this attention paid to what seems to trouble us? Frankly, I find it a shame. Because we all know how magical teaching can be. Those moments where we see that lightbulb go off in a child's mind are pure joy. When we've watched a child struggle and struggle with something and then it just clicks! These moments are priceless. When we witness a student who, for whatever reason, believed he was not smart have one of those transformative experiences where he sees his potential and begins to shift his entire perspective of himself—these moments stay with us forever. When we observe a student get so absorbed in her learning, so fascinated by what she's discovered that she emerges with an idea entirely new to her—these moments are why we do this. It's when we choose to keep our focus on the problems that we lose sight of the joys of teaching.

I was a public school teacher for ten years. For the past ten years, I've been a literacy strategist and coach helping educators advance rigorous and relevant instructional design and learning in classrooms. My work affords me the opportunity to fly all over the country and meet educators at all stages of experience and who teach across grade levels and disciplines. I've had countless conversations with hundreds, perhaps thousands of teachers. I've heard their frustrations and concerns. I've also, unfortunately, heard many express a sense of hopelessness in figuring out how to meet the needs of all of our students. Some believe our challenges are so deep that we'll never be able to dig out from them.

I disagree. I am not hopeless. From all my conversations, I have come to believe something else is going on: we're focusing too heavily on that which we, the individual educators, cannot change.

We're overwhelmed by the problems we're told we have, many of which are made and fixed far outside our classrooms. We're inundated with a constant stream of new learning theories, the latest instructional techniques, even old principles of pedagogy that are new again. We suffer from initiative overload. Our heads are spinning as we try to keep up. We're so besieged by standards, strategies, and structures that we feel forced to be reactive, not proactive, in the classroom.

From this frantic state of mind, it's common to focus exclusively on the little things, the tactics, the techniques. In the overwhelmed moment, it feels easier to think small because it feels too daunting to slow down and think big. But in our guts, we know this approach will not work over the long term. We begin to feel ineffective because we know we're merely throwing darts at the wall and hoping one of them will stick. It's a maddening feeling, one that most of us have experienced at some point. When we are mired in the details, we feel we have no time to step back, look at the bigger picture, and then form a cohesive plan aimed at achieving a specific goal.

I know this frustration. I know it because I've been there, and I have teachers vent regularly to me that they feel stuck in the mud, unable to see the forest for the trees. When you express your frustrations to me, I hear you. When you reiterate the very real difficulty of learning and applying yet more instructional strategies and tactics given the realities of your classroom, I am listening. I *know* the realities of the classroom. I was in that classroom! Teaching to students from a broad swath of cultures, at every level of aptitude, and across a spectrum of needs is difficult, period. It is difficult for those just starting out. It is difficult for the most seasoned of teachers.

Yet, we achieve little by talking too much about how difficult it is. I see two common cases and consequences of problem-fixation:

1. Teachers feel so consumed by the problems in their own classrooms that they shut the door—literally and figuratively— in a sort of attempt to contain their problems and keep the problems *out there* from seeping in. But inadvertently, they also shut out available supports and productive collaboration partners.
2. Teachers feel so defeated by the problems plaguing our education system on the national level that they begin to believe there's little that can be done in the classroom to move the needle.

In both cases, I think we're missing the point. The point is that when we focus on our problems, no matter what we perceive them to be, we keep them active, present, and in our way. It's paralyzing and counterproductive.

Instead, I encourage you to reset your focus on where you have the power to make change. Spend your time thinking about what's in your control to influence. Ponder how you can make strategic decisions with colleagues and community members who share your desire to find direct-impact solutions to the issues within your reach to tackle. Collaborate with those who will support and reinforce improvements in your classroom and do the same for them. Begin where you are: in your classroom and in your school, in front of the very people who matter above all in the education system, the very people who need you most—your students.

This book is for the educator who understands the enormity of our challenges, but prefers to focus on what is positive and hopeful in our world as educators. This book is for the teacher who wants to focus on changing what can be changed and not get distracted by what cannot be changed. This book is for the educator eager for simple—yes, simple— and useful ideas, strategies, and tactics to move through our challenges and choose solutions that drive impact in our students' lives. This book is for the teacher who seeks to cut through the noise and cut to the chase. Perhaps most importantly, this book is for the teacher who craves more of those moments of pure teaching joy and who recognizes the unique power teachers can have in shaping the paths students chart for themselves.

As an art student at Simpson College, George Washington Carver studied under a teacher named Etta May Budd. In a 1922 letter Carver wrote to a botany professor at Iowa State University, he said: "I am greatly indebted [to Miss Etta M. Budd] for whatever measure of success that has come to me" (Carver, 1922). By all accounts, when it came to her students, Budd didn't think of them exclusively as art students, but as multifaceted people with futures and realities ahead of them. Budd recognized an incredible attention to detail and precision in Carver's paintings of plant life. She also recognized that no matter the level of talent, an African-American man at that time pursuing an art career would be doomed to a life of poverty. So, Budd nudged Carver to apply his love of plants more relevantly to a career in agriculture. It was Budd who suggested to Carver that he apply to Iowa State Agricultural School (now Iowa State University) and study botany (Vella, 2015).

Even George Washington Carver needed the support, guidance, and encouragement of teachers.

How can we become the kind of teachers who recognize each student's potential and then purposely move to nurture, not stymie it? How do we make those magical, joy-of-teaching moments a regular occurrence in our classrooms?

To get there, we have to slow down. We have to simplify things, get back to the basics, change our brains, shift our perspectives, adopt a Quad D attitude. It is only from there—from a new mindset rooted in a few simple overarching principles—that we can begin to make strategic decisions. It is only with a Quad D attitude that we can apply intentional instructional design to our classrooms for the express purpose of advancing the goals we have for ourselves and our students. We have to slow down to speed up. This book is designed to help you do just that. Let's start by getting simple.

KISS Your Brain Part 1: Keep It Simple

I often like to say, "KISS Your Brain." But my version of KISS wouldn't dare call anyone stupid. Keep it simple, yes, but that second "S" is for *strategic*. Keep it simple and strategic.

KISS Your Brain is meant to remind you that the simplest solution is often the most effective one. It's also meant to help you develop a habit of thinking and making decisions from a strategic mindset.

Let's first dig into the simplicity aspect.

Isaac Newton said, "Truth is ever to be found in simplicity, and not in the multiplicity and confusion of things." I couldn't agree more. From my experience, the power of the Rigor/Relevance Framework is its simplicity. Two axes, four quadrants, and an entire framework through which to consider instruction and learning. It's straightforward and that's what makes it effective.

The educators I work with grasp rigor and relevance on an intellectual level. The rubrics are enlightening when it comes to evaluating the depth of rigor, the breadth of relevance, and the level of engagement in a classroom. But it is challenging to translate a framework and rubrics, no matter how to the point they may be, into *actionable* intentional instructional design and usable classroom tools and techniques. We all understand what it means for students to synthesize information. But how can we actually get them to do this? We all know what it means for students to create something. But what kinds of tasks will actually elicit creativity and originality?

When I began to think about writing this book, I knew that I wanted to put rigor, relevance, and engagement in simple, digestible terms. I wanted to do this for two reasons.

First, if we could think about rigor, relevance, and engagement in more familiar terms, we could help eliminate the gap between framework and instructional design. This gap exists because the Framework and rubrics are conceptual and by definition not applied, but instructional design is tangible and applied. It's difficult to draw action from theory. My thinking—and my intention—was that if we can think of rigor, relevance, and engagement as actionable ideas, ideas that we already regularly use in our own lives, then we are empowered to move from concept to creation and close the gap.

The second reason I wanted to distill rigor, relevance, and engagement to their respective cores is because of the primary rule of engagement: the most surefire way to engage your students in a rigorous and relevant education is to *invite* them into it.

I have seen this again and again. The classrooms with the students who are most engaged in rigorous and relevant learning are those where students know exactly what the Rigor/Relevance Framework is. They are made fully aware that rigorous and relevant thinking and doing are the goal in the classroom. By being included in the process, by being informed about its components and how it works, these students feel entrusted with a shared responsibility in their learning. They feel as though they are a *part of* their education, not simply on the receiving end of it. They are empowered, motivated, and accountable. They are *engaged*.

In this book, it is my specific aim to provide you with a way to think about and talk about the Rigor/Relevance Framework and its corresponding rubrics in terms simple enough that even the youngest children will understand. Share with your students what you cull from this book. Explain rigor, relevance, and learner engagement to them in words and ideas that they will find familiar—and hopefully interesting and fun. Invite them in, and let them know why. In doing so, you will naturally engage them.

Keep it simple. And also strategic.

KISS Your Brain Part 2: Keep It Strategic

The word *strategy* is overused and often misused. In most cases, it's not a huge deal. But if we want to make a habit of KISSing our brains, this is one of those situations where getting clear on what a strategy is matters.

A goal is that thing we hope to achieve. A strategy is *how* we're going to achieve that goal. Tactics are the *what*, the action or actions we're going to take to advance the strategy to, in turn, achieve the goal.

Our goal is a Quad D environment where students are engaged in rigorous and relevant learning. The nine indicators of the rubrics—High-Level Questioning, Academic Discussion, Thoughtful Work, Meaningful Work, Authentic Resources, Learning Connections, Active Participation, Learning Environment, and Formative Processes and Tools—are the how. How are we going to keep ourselves on track to achieve this goal? By intentionally designing instruction and student tasks that consider all nine indicators of rigor, relevance, and engagement. This is the second "S" in KISS Your Brain. By addressing these nine rubric indicators, our instructional planning will naturally be devised through a strategic lens. The instruction techniques, tools, tasks, anything you put in your toolbox of classroom activities—these are the tactics (and for our purposes, they are synonyms). They are the *what*. They are what we are going to do in the classroom to make sure we're addressing all nine rubric indicators with regularity. And they are only as worthwhile as their ability to support our strategies and goals.

Strategic teaching means intentionally designing instruction to move closer and closer to the goal. Intentionality is key to strategy. Without intentionality, there can be no strategy. If we don't design our instruction with the end goal in mind, then we risk letting our classrooms drift into an aimless wasteland of low rigor and irrelevance. Without a goal and a strategy to get you there, what guides your decisions, your tactics? What fills your class time? In my experience, the answers to these questions are "nothing" and "busy work." Without a goal and a strategy to get you there, what motivates your students? What are they working toward? In my experience, the answers to these questions are "nothing" and "no one knows." In these cases, everyone's time is wasted, yours too, and to devastating effects and missed opportunities.

Remember that frantic, reactive mindset? Those whose heads are spinning from overload? Watch and you will notice that those in this unfortunate position typically all begin to do the same thing: they devolve to being merely tactical, not strategic. Desperate for some sense of control or progress, no matter how fleeting or minimal, they focus only on the tactics without first ensuring that they support a strategy and goal. In the moment, grasping for little things just to fill class time feels easier. People can even convince themselves it feels necessary. But that is defensive, survival-mode thinking that will only keep them stuck spinning their wheels in tactical muck. The only way to get out of the mud is to slow down. Set a goal. Devise a strategy. And then choose and create the tactics that support the strategy. Only then are we fully out of the mud, trucking along Rigor and Relevance Road toward our Quad D destination.

Start with the end in mind. Keep it simple. Keep it strategic. Then get moving.

Begin Where You Are. Just Be Sure to Begin.

I believe wholeheartedly in the Rigor/Relevance Framework. I have seen its steadfast application in the classroom transform dull learning environments into ones that energize, excite, and enliven students. My collection of stories of how the Framework pulled teachers and students out from the wasteland of low rigor and low relevance and into learning that is fun, multi-dimensional, relatable, and interesting to students is too numerous to count. I've witnessed hundreds of occasions where the Framework has been that vehicle that lifted students from a lack of faith in themselves and into a place of confidence in their capacity to rise to high expectations. There's a long list of powerful learning constructs out there that can change lives, and I know the Framework to be one of them.

I also believe that a sole and exclusive focus on getting to Quad D instruction and learning is not sufficient. It can even be a little self-defeating. Do not get me wrong: it is absolutely necessary, but it cannot start and end with just Quad D. We constantly hear the importance of scaffolding learning for our students. Why would we, the adults, not also benefit from scaffolding? Scaffolding is a smart learning strategy no matter the learner's age.

To expect that the teacher new to the Framework achieve a Quad D classroom right out of the gate is unrealistic. Such a notion puts too much pressure on the teacher. We are human; when we feel we are asked to accomplish something in an unrealistic timeline without an opportunity to study, learn, and improve, a natural response is to give up. We feel set up to fail, so we default to our old ways. The devil we know is better than the devil taunting us to pull off something that feels impossible.

I encourage you to become a student of the Rigor/Relevance Framework—the operative word being *student*. The goal on day one is not to be some sort of Quad D Jedi master. It's simply to *move beyond* Quad A. That's it. Just start moving. I know this from observing classroom after classroom, so please trust me when I say that the mere act of putting effort into moving beyond Quad A is, by definition, a Quad D exercise. It stems from a Quad D mindset. It is the behavior of someone who has set a high bar and an ambitious goal, and then crafted a realistic plan to get there—one step at a time.

If our choice is either to magically create Quad D classrooms on day one or to invite our students to learn the Framework along with us, step by step, obviously the latter is the superior choice! In the former choice, the students are blindsided by rapid change that they don't fully understand, and they tend to freeze. Typically out of frustration, the teacher gives up and resorts to past patterns. In the latter choice, the teacher is not only scaffolding the Framework for herself, but also for her students. This is not a waste of students' time. Eventually, with patience and practice, intentional Quad D instructional design will become second nature to you and you'll find you're applying multiple tools of rigor and relevance throughout a class with ease. But until you get there, please know that scaffolding your learning in front of and with your students is a powerful opportunity to mirror to them what commitment, effort, productive struggle, and growth look like. Talk about practicing what you preach!

When it comes to the Framework, you have a choice. You can expect some sort of overnight magical Quad D transformation, or you can be realistic and let yourself learn. From my years of experience, I know without a doubt that the choice with the highest success rate is to begin simply by moving beyond Quad A.

You have a goal. You have your strategic lens on. You are keeping it simple. The next step is simply to begin where you are. If that means your first step is to move beyond Quad A, great, then that's the plan. With practice and time, you will find yourself moving into Quad B, if your focus is to extend relevance out of Quad A. Or you will find you have moved into Quad C, if your intention has been to raise rigor beyond Quad A. Both are excellent, necessary goals and achievements. Once you get comfortable moving to Quads B and C, begin trying to toggle between raising rigor and extending relevance throughout one class session. And now, dear student of the Rigor/Relevance Framework, you are officially moving toward Quad D. And then one day, you find yourself naturally advancing rigor and relevance simultaneously. You have reached Quad D. And then you do it again, and again. And eventually you find yourself in Quad D with ease and regularity.

But nothing in life is constant. Some new content, standard, or technology will come along, and you will have to repeat the process from the start, beginning by just moving beyond Quad A. All the while, please rest assured; the mere commitment to your goal, no matter where on the progress line you are, will set a Quad D tone in your classroom that your students will *feel*. They will begin to grasp what it means to embody Quad D, to approach everything with a Quad D attitude. They will witness what hard work, resilience, and progress look like—and the rewards they can yield—from a Quad D mindset.

Would we ever tell our students there's shame in step-stoning their way to meet a goal? Absolutely not. Would we ever suggest to them that once they get enough A-pluses or gain enough experience, they will no longer need to learn more? We know that's absurd. A Quad D mindset means learning is lifelong. Mirroring the behavior we want our students to exhibit is one of the most effective teaching tools out there.

To that end, let's capture the Quad D spirit of George Washington Carver and get curious about what drives rigor, relevance, and engagement. Let's imagine what these concepts will look like when brought to life in our classrooms. And let's exercise our agency, our power, and choose to be the kind of teacher that changes and improves lives.

Chapter Two

Curiosity: Why Rigor Matters

A sense of curiosity is nature's original school of education.
—Smiley Blanton

Step Away from the Smartphone

A challenge: in the next couple of days, keep count of how many times you reach for your smartphone the second a question comes up. Any question. Who was the president at the turn of the twentieth century? What was that actor's name in that movie that won best picture? How do I get to that restaurant? What's the capital of that country?

Sure, there are times where asking Google a question is the best option. For instance, "What's a 10-minute chicken recipe?" is a question where the limits of your culinary knowledge are your limits, and no amount of reasoning will do much good (and could also lead you down the path to a dinner no one wants to touch).

Yet, in most cases, when we reflexively reach for our smartphones, we reach for the easy way out. We miss an opportunity to work our brain, to use our recall muscle, and to strengthen those neural pathways that connect bits of information that help us arrive at a justified answer.

The risks, though, are greater than that, greater than just a missed opportunity here and there for a little cognitive exercise.

In short, when we go to our smartphones to be reminded who was president in 1900, we cut the link between curiosity and effort. When we do this again and again and again, we habituate ourselves out of asking questions and thinking through things. Put another way, we begin to lose something we were born with: curiosity.

As babies who came into this world knowing absolutely nothing of it, curiosity was our only tool and our survival technique. We explore at first through our senses. We touch whatever we can, we put anything and everything in our mouths, we smell and react, we fix our gaze on intriguing objects, we listen and begin to mimic sounds. And then, as we begin to get language, questions naturally follow—40,000 of them between the ages of three and five by one estimation (Leslie, 2014). Questions become the way we follow our curiosity to explore and get to know our world so that we can grasp how to function, survive, and thrive.

Anyone who has spent time with toddlers knows how much they love to ask questions. Surely, this practice loses its charm as the number of questions ticks up. So much so that perhaps we've all been guilty of telling those precious little question machines to give us a break already! What's happening here, though, is significant in the development of a child's entire approach to the world. When the child's questions shift from "what" to "why," we're witnessing what psychologists call a change from "diversive" curiosity to "epistemic" curiosity (Leslie, 2015).

Diversive curiosity is that need for novelty or new experience. It's what causes you to visit a new restaurant or city, or click on an intriguing headline. It's generally shallow and surface. While important, diversive curiosity can be satisfied with (ahem) a quick query on a smartphone. Epistemic curiosity is more sophisticated. It's what drives a deeper quest for knowledge and a desire to grasp how seemingly disparate bits of information come together, or even better, a desire to put seemingly disparate bits of information together on your own to create a new idea. When you want to analyze and evaluate something to a point of high-level understanding and creation of new thoughts, you are following your epistemic curiosity.

While epistemic curiosity is the brand of curiosity that leads to rich learning and meaningful engagement with information, diversive curiosity serves an important purpose. Diversive curiosity is often the conduit to epistemic curiosity, and thus advanced learning. Consider the question, "Who was president in 1900?" If you resist the urge to consult your phone, you'll have to ask some questions to get the wheels in your brain turning.

What was going on in America at the turn of the century? What significant economic, social, or global events were happening at the time? Was there any unrest? Who were other presidents around the time? What preceded 1900 historically and what notable events followed? We were following on the heels of an economic downturn and the Spanish-American War. The Industrial Revolution was underfoot, which meant the country was undergoing enormous economic and social change. Wait a minute, wasn't a president assassinated around that time?

Going through such questions in search of clues that might trigger your memory into delivering the fact that William McKinley was president in 1900 (only to be assassinated a year later, just barely into his second term) has another effect. It might lead you to be curious about any number of things around the McKinley presidency. And then your epistemic curiosity is off and running. Who knows where that can take you, beyond the certainty that it will result in, at least, more knowledge and some context on McKinley's untimely demise.

Curiosity is triggered when you confront a gap in knowledge. This implies that some degree of knowledge, however small, is a prerequisite to curiosity. If this is true, then the more you know, the more you begin to see you don't know, and the more you want to know (Leslie, 2015).

Do you see now the risks of always reaching for your smartphone to do your thinking for you? Slowly but surely you will dull your natural-born desire to ask what *and* why.

This is all well and good, you might be thinking. We should all try to reach for our smartphones a little less and reach into our brains a little more, got it. But what does this have to do with us as educators? Everything.

What Is Academic Rigor?

Curiosity is a willing, a proud, an eager confession of ignorance. —S. Leonard Rubinstein

As a public school teacher for 10 years and now a literacy strategist and coach who helps educators advance rigorous and relevant instructional design and learning in classrooms across the country, I repeatedly run into a common issue: people often struggle to grasp what rigor means in practice in the classroom. Of course we all know what the word *rigor* means. But as a learning construct, it becomes somewhat more abstract and conceptual, which can make it difficult for educators to translate meaning into concrete instructional strategies and tactics to advance rigorous learning.

I've found that stepping out of the dictionary and stepping into analogy to explain rigorous learning helps turn on that lightbulb.

On the Rigor/Relevance Framework, rigor is captured on the thinking continuum (vertical axis) and uses the revised Bloom's Taxonomy to define levels of thinking from least to most complex: Remembering, Understanding, Applying, Analyzing, Evaluating, and Creating (Anderson & Krathwohl, 2001).

Rigor/Relevance Framework®

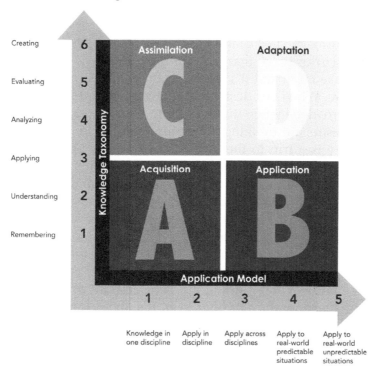

A	B	C	D
Students gather and store bits of knowledge and information. Students are primarily expected to remember or understand this knowledge.	Students use acquired knowledge to solve problems, design solutions, and complete work. The highest level of application is to apply knowledge to new and unpredictable situations.	Students extend and refine their acquired knowledge to be able to use that knowledge automatically and routinely to analyze and solve problems and create solutions.	Students think in complex ways and can apply their knowledge and skills. Even when confronted with perplexing unknowns, students can create solutions and take action that further develops their skills and knowledge.

To understand the notion of guiding students up the rigor axis, it helps to understand what drives that trip up the axis, that tangible idea that can move us from concept to creation—and that is curiosity. Curiosity is that actionable idea we can use to imagine, create, and recognize tactics and techniques that will promote rigor in our classrooms. Curiosity is defined by Merriam-Webster as, simply "the desire to learn or know more about something or someone," with intellectual curiosity specifically noted as "interest leading to inquiry." At its core, curiosity is that natural pull to know more. Add the intellectual take on it, and it's the willingness to ask questions to get at knowing more. When our desire to know more about something grows deeper and broader—when it moves from diverse to epistemic—if we follow that desire, our thinking will naturally move up the rigor axis.

If curiosity is a trip to the gym to exercise our brains, rigor is the amount of weight we're loading up on the barbell. It's how challenging and probing a question is, or how enriching and multifaceted a discussion is, or how much room an assignment leaves for exploration and discovery. It's a function of both how clear the seed of a learning task is and how much space it leaves for a flower to blossom.

Rigor is not about stumping the student. Put another way, it's not about asking a novice weightlifter to bench press 300 pounds on the first day. But it's also not about lifting the same amount of weight day after day, month after month, year after year. It's about starting with a little bit of weight and building, while still challenging the person to improve every day, to keep adding a few more pounds. It's inciting curiosity and then guiding students through the process of following that curiosity to broader and more expansive places, as the thought process, all the while, moves from simple to complex.

To enhance rigor in the classroom is to stoke epistemic curiosity. Moving your students up the rigor scale is a matter of creating a learning environment where curiosity of all stripes is encouraged, purposefully stimulated, nurtured, and supported. From there, it requires intentionally designing instruction to achieve these things. In the rigorous classroom, the conversation starts by asking who was president at the beginning of the twentieth century, and ends, as an example, in a discussion about the parallels that can be drawn between events then and events today, and what that might mean in terms of our society, or our economy, or our next election cycle. And in the *strategically* rigorous classroom, the arc of this exercise is entirely pre-planned, on purpose, and not left to chance.

As we've discussed, there is always a time and place for diversive curiosity. It can serve as a baseline, a launching pad for epistemic curiosity to take flight and bring increasingly rigorous thought along for the ride. As teachers, it's our job to stimulate that epistemic curiosity whenever possible. Because what we're really trying to do is create a *habit* of curiosity. If students are habituated to let their minds explore, wonder, ponder, and then seek more and more knowledge, the benefits will span their entire professional and personal lives.

Students regularly exposed to purposeful opportunities for rigorous thinking will make greater and more frequent leaps in learning. Their performance in school will improve. Over time, these students stand a greater chance of having more post-secondary opportunities, with a higher likelihood of excelling in the paths they choose. From there, these students will face more career prospects and greater earning power.

In his book *Curious: The Desire to Know and Why Your Future Depends on It*, Ian Leslie explains what it takes to succeed in the high-paying jobs of the twenty-first century. As the world gets more complex, fast-paced, and globalized, high-paying jobs will increasingly rely on strong collaboration skills. We often hear of the divide between those who do and do not win the higher-paying, higher-skill jobs as the skills gap, or the wage gap. Leslie calls it the "curiosity gap" because to him, those who land the high-paying jobs are going to be those who regularly practice epistemic curiosity, which can directly improve collaborative skills (Leslie, 2015).

To Leslie, the most effective collaborators are those who are both generalists and specialists, those who are expert in something specific, but also have knowledge about the surrounding components of the company or industry. The engineer can collaborate most effectively with the product designer, marketer, accountant, and sales rep if she understands a little about each of those other jobs. If the engineer has familiarized herself with consumer use preferences (e.g., the customer prefers a dial to a button), marketing circumstances (e.g., it's easier to market a product of this size and weight), budgetary constraints (e.g., this material is cheaper than that material), and sales considerations (e.g., sales reps had more success selling this product to stores than that other product), then the engineer stands the best shot of building a product that the company stands most likely to sell well. Her impact on the company's goals and bottom line is then direct and strong (Leslie, 2015).

Leslie identifies a third kind of curiosity in his book that underpins the most productive collaborations and is a byproduct of a habit of epistemic curiosity: empathic curiosity. When you are curious about another person's experience, when you stop to ask questions about what this or that might feel like to another person, you develop empathy. Anyone who's ever had a friendship or relationship of any kind knows that empathy is key to mutually respectful, dynamic, fulfilling, and healthy connections (Leslie, 2015).

That curiosity can lead to empathy is why psychologist Todd Kashdan believes curiosity is not only a driving force behind a lifelong interest in learning, but it's also a driver behind connection and well-being. The curious will inevitably find that their curiosity will put them in front of new people. The curious will find themselves forging new connections and relationships, and their empathy will allow those connections to become strong and healthy (Kashdan, 2009).

To Kashdan, curiosity is also about being able to confront uncertainty with a positive attitude. I like to think of it more as confronting uncertainty with a toolbox in hand. For those of us who've had our curiosity supported and nurtured, we know what to do when we confront uncertainty, which we will do inevitably and repeatedly throughout life. We know to begin by asking thoughtful questions, then analyzing the situation, then processing the information we know and don't know, and then making an evaluative judgment call about how best to navigate through the uncertainty. We have a roadmap for rigorously considering possible outcomes and a path forward.

Hopefully by now the link between curiosity and rigor is clear and convincing. Hopefully by now you see that to drive rigor in the classroom requires intentionally creating opportunities for diverse and epistemic curiosity and then supporting students on their paths of discovery as they follow that curiosity. And hopefully I have made you a believer in the idea that by helping our students develop a habit of curiosity, we are helping them gain the tools to achieve in school, careers, and life. To begin, we must do what we can to keep our own curiosity alive.

Step away from the smartphone.

From there, the Rigor Rubric provides three indicators of intentionally rigorous instructional design and student learning: High-Level Questioning, Thoughtful Work, and Academic Discussion.

The order in which you plan for well-developed levels of rigor through these indicators is often a function of how you prefer to work, what the content is, or what you hope to achieve in a particular module. However you start, you'll soon find that most tactics facilitate rigor within multiple indicators at once. They all play off of and enhance each other. What matters to begin is coming up with a worthy topic or learning source and then designing instruction around it that is rigorous across all three indicators.

Are you curious about how to do this? Good. Let's start with questions.

Rigor Indicator: High-Level Questioning

Judge a man by his questions rather than by his answers.
—Voltaire

A question for you about your relationship with questions: How willing are you to ask questions out loud, in front of colleagues or peers? How often do you hold back from asking a question in public out of a concern you'll look ignorant, particularly about something you worry others will think you should know? Eventually, as adults, we find ourselves unwilling to admit knowledge gaps and keep questions to ourselves. Behind this fact is another one: curiosity is all too often perceived as something appropriate only for small children.

Once children start advancing in grade levels, we see the rate of student questions drop off (Leslie, 2015). This could be because students are so focused on content and retaining knowledge. Or it could be because in the inherently competitive and vulnerable environment that the classroom can be, students begin to feel shy about asking questions out of concern their classmates might think they're stupid. And the slow socialization out of curiosity begins. Whatever the reason, developing a fear of asking questions is a problem.

As teachers—stewards of students going through the normal insecurities and self-consciousness of childhood—it is very much our problem.

The student learns how to ask high-level questions by repeat exposure to high-level questions. It's the job of the teacher first to model high-level questions—those that elicit deeper thinking and thoughtful responses—and then summon them from students themselves. As teachers, we need to make questions frequent, welcome, and acceptable in the classroom. It must be said and shown to students that questions are powerful learning tools and should be used anytime they confront an information gap. After all, what happens when we face a learning gap and do the research or inquiry to fill it? We gain more knowledge, which makes us want to gain yet more knowledge. For this to happen, we have to make students feel safe asking questions. If they don't, they won't. The short-term and long-term consequences of the child who stops asking questions, who stops being curious, are many and real.

First, academic performance begins to suffer. Then post-secondary prospects shrink. Then career prospects dwindle. And on and on. But it's not just academic and career performance that are in question when it comes to, well, a habit of asking meaningful questions. Asking questions beyond the facts at hand can make or break a child's long-term prospects in another surprising way. And it has much to do with brain development.

Consider the seventh-grader attending a party. He is confronted with an opportunity to drink alcohol. Opportunity and access turn into peer pressure. Peer pressure turns into caving in. This, of course, can then go many ways. A few sips and nothing more, not to be repeated again. Or the slow building of a habit as a regular means of socializing. From that point, what happens is a matter of chance—getting caught or not. Getting caught drinking under age, getting caught driving under the influence, getting caught with suffering school performance, getting caught up in the wrong crowd. And it all begins with that first encounter with peer pressure to engage in illegal or dangerous behavior.

What's significant here is the child's brain. In the fully formed brain, decisions are made in the prefrontal cortex, which is the rational part of the brain. The prefrontal cortex provides a person the ability to think through circumstances, imagine different possible scenarios and outcomes that could stem from one event, and consider long-term consequences. It's the place in the brain where good judgment comes from (University of Rochester Medical Center, n.d.).

Interestingly, and challengingly, the prefrontal cortex is not fully developed until around age 25. Up to that point, a person processes information in the amygdale, the emotional part of the brain. It's no wonder teens are so susceptible to peer pressure.

Clearly, though, not every child is at the mercy of his or her emotional brain, or else many more would end up on a troubled path, and, in worst-case scenarios, fundamentally altering their paths in life. Why, then, do so many kids have the ability to pause and consider the long-term consequences when pressured to take part in bad behavior?

Questions. The child who's developed the habit of asking probing questions will be more prepared to handle peer pressure. He will have the tools to pause and ask himself questions such as: "What happens if I take this sip of alcohol? What happens if my parents find out? Or if the police show up? What happens if my school finds out? What happens if I end up in the car with someone who's been drinking?" By being trained to ask thoughtful questions and look beyond the information he has up to this point, this child's brain will have a tool to compensate for its developmental limitations. This can only be taught.

As a component of a rigorous learning environment, high-level and thoughtful questions cannot be understated. They matter for success in school and an ability to build (and build upon) knowledge, to analyze, and to evaluate information from myriad angles, and then to connect dots to achieve new understanding. They matter for winning great jobs and creating careers that allow for self-sustainability. But their significance far exceeds what happens in school and jobs. They matter for children whose brains lack a literal ability to consider long-term consequences of actions that can permanently change the course of their lives.

As teachers, we must protect, nurture, and encourage curiosity. This involves acknowledging that questions are linchpins of learning, not indicators of ignorance. We need to say out loud to our students that gaps in knowledge are the drivers of our natural-born curiosity, not anything to be ashamed of. And we must reiterate to them that more important than knowledge is the desire to get knowledge.

From there, it's up to us to model high-level questions, leaving space and time for students to reflect before answering. While recall questions have their place in scaffolding thought, more rigorous questions require analysis from students. They push students to differentiate between relevant and irrelevant details when forming an answer. From there, rigorous questions challenge students to synthesize and merge bits of information to generate new thoughts, ideas, or even questions and evaluate them against a certain focus, context, or learning goal. In the well-developed classroom, eventually we leave it to the students to ask the rigorous questions of each other.

Let's make a commitment to destigmatize questions in the classroom. Let's tell our students that questions are the difference between a one-dimensional world and a three-dimensional world. Questions are the key that unlocks the door to understanding events, ideas, people, and circumstances on a far more relevant, interesting, fun, and sophisticated level. Questions are what take us out of a black-and-white world and move us into an exhilarating Technicolor one.

Okay, I recognize my language might be getting a little dramatic. But it's merely to drive home the transformative power that high-level questioning can, and needs to, have in our classrooms. While all nine indicators of the Rigor, Relevance, and Engagement rubrics are equally important, high-level questioning has a uniquely foundational role.

Not to mention, great questions make for the most engaging and memorable conversations.

Rigor Indicator: Academic Discussion

A conversation is a dialogue, not a monologue.
—Truman Capote

Think about the last exhilarating conversation you had. One of those dynamic conversations that left you buzzing with satisfaction and new ideas. Maybe it was with a spouse, a coworker, or even with some friends over a meal. What made it so invigorating?

Odds are, it challenged your thinking in some way, however minimally, and left you pondering the topics covered even after the dialogue ended. The conversation *went* someplace. It didn't just rehash what was already known, but it took something at least in part known and then led to a new place as yet undiscovered by you. It left you buzzing because it's thrilling to uncover uncharted spaces in our brains that then seek to be filled. You know what I'm going to say here, right? The conversation was so satisfying because it stoked your epistemic curiosity.

These are the types of discussions we want to replicate in our classrooms with regularity. They typically require scaffolding to get there, so some conversations must necessarily be a bit simpler and more explanatory to work up to those that leave students abuzz with new knowledge and thoughts. But that conversation you had over dinner with your closest friends that left you so intellectually fulfilled? That's what we're aiming for in our classrooms, just with relevant, content-specific topics on the agenda and an intentional use of academic language and rich vocabulary.

When you think about those types of conversations, part of what is so engaging about them is that they progress organically. This point spurs this thought, which leads to that question, which then leaps to that idea. Sometimes the content of the conversation can veer far off course, and someone has to bring everyone else back to the larger point. But these conversations have a life to them, a sort of boundlessness where people are welcome to say what comes to their minds and see where it goes. It's typically openness that allows for and results in the new ideas, thoughts, and perspectives that conversation participants can walk away with and then continue to reflect upon on their own.

To capture this in the classroom, we have to intentionally utilize a discussion structure that is both focused and open. As teachers, we play the role of providing the focus. We then hand it over to students to follow where their curiosity about the focused topic takes them. When we see that the conversation has veered too far off track, we rein it back in with a pre-planned statement to refocus everyone. When we feel that the class has collectively grasped a stepping stone concept, we interject as needed with pre-planned high-level questions, learning tasks, or techniques to help move the discussion up the rigor axis.

All the while, we must keep the room safe. We must be recognize when there are too few questions and then remind everyone that we are a room of lifelong learners who know questions are the water that makes the seed of curiosity grow. Our aim is to know that every student feels a part of the conversation and so we apply techniques when needed to involve those who haven't yet participated. If we see a disrespectful response to a question, opinion, thought, or idea, we remind our students that big ideas are born from lots of little ones, and any little thought or idea can be that thing that triggers the big one.

When it comes to rigorous academic discussion that allows curiosity to thrive and drive the conversation and leaves students abuzz with new thoughts, we as teachers are acting primarily as coaches. We're cultivating the attitudes that will make for a team approach to a great game. Then we let the players play the game, making sure each gets a chance on the field. We guide them toward advancing up the field and give pointers when progress stalls. Like any effective coach, prior to the game, we have to have a playbook or a script in place to prime everyone for and guide them through a spirited interaction.

Rigor Indicator: Thoughtful Work

If everyone is thinking alike, then somebody isn't thinking.
—George S. Patton

Thoughtful work. Let's call this one what it is: tricky. Admittedly, thoughtful work can seem abstract. Yet it's critical to creating opportunities for rigor. So before we get into the nuts and bolts of what thoughtful work looks like in the classroom, I find it helpful to ground thinking about thoughtful work in an idea we're all familiar with.

A superior asks you to take lead on a project. The end goal is to propose a detailed, research-backed plan to increase community engagement through schoolwide learning opportunities. To do this, you'll need to build a team capable not only of devising a plan to invite members of the community into student learning, but also of determining the best approach to tackle this project. Your superior put you at the helm because you've been creative and successful in involving the community in your own classroom. You've experimented and begun to understand what works and what doesn't when attempting to engage those beyond school walls. You've received feedback from both students and community members around their preferences when collaborating. You've also taken care to cultivate many professional relationships and now have a community network you can tap into for research. Additionally, you've collaborated with a few teachers in some of your community learning programs and you've gotten a sense of their strengths and passions. Other teachers have expressed an interest in collaborating with you, as well. Not inconsequentially, you know which teachers are resistant to involving the community in their classrooms and wonder if you now have an opportunity to change some of their minds by empowering them to help out.

You're honored to have been selected to lead this project. You're excited because you care about it deeply. You know you have unique experience that will help your team hit the ground running. You can't wait to get started and hit a home run.

What if, though, your superior also insisted that you can only have three people working with you, and two of them must be teacher A and teacher B. She also expresses a preference for how you should delegate the work amongst the team. And what if she told you that you really shouldn't tap into your community network, as it might appear unprofessional to approach them for their ideas rather than a specific request to collaborate on a learning module. Finally, she wants you to come to her immediately when you hit any issues, no matter how small.

All of a sudden, you're not so excited. Arbitrary limits to the potential success of this project have been put on it before it has even begun. You've been stripped of your autonomy. You think the team needs to be larger, and you're also confident that those two teachers who have to be on the team will not take a serious interest in it. You've spent so much time nurturing certain relationships with community members for this exact reason—so that you could feel comfortable asking them for their opinions now and then. You know they hold valuable insights that will allow you to build the best community engagement program possible. You can already tell that the bounds put on the project will hinder the creation of new and original ideas. You feel stymied, frustrated, and unmotivated. If only your superior trusted you enough to provide the freedom necessary for you to tackle this project in a way that will be most motivating, interesting, and productive for everyone involved, you know you and your team would do a bang-up job.

In his book *Drive: The Surprising Truth About What Motivates Us*, Daniel Pink uses research to show that our standard employee motivation system is outdated. The typical carrot-and-stick approach to motivation works only in simple, routine work with a clear solution: do X to get Y. It does not motivate people who work under complex, ambiguous circumstances. According to Pink, to motivate people in the twenty-first century, work needs to enable a person's natural desire for mastery, purpose, and autonomy (Pink, 2011). To him, the driver of autonomy is the ability to self-direct and use discovery to forge the most efficient and appropriate path forward.

Thoughtful work supports that desire for self-direction and self-discovery, while also preparing students for complex, ambiguous, real-world tasks. Thoughtful work is work that hits that sweet spot between just enough structure and just enough freedom. In this admittedly not-quite-perfect analogy (because children require more guidance in the learning process than experienced adults likely would), had the superior stopped short of putting strict guidelines on the teacher that didn't take into account the teacher's insights and informed preferences, then the teacher would have been able to go about the project from the sweet spot. She would have been able to apply her knowledge to develop the most logical plan of attack. She then would have been able to recognize when the plan presented limits or roadblocks, and she would have had the space to adapt and change course accordingly or approach her superior for help where necessary. She and her team would have been given ample runway for creativity to take flight. All the while, she would remain engaged and motivated—because, after all, with freedom comes ownership and accountability.

In general terms, thoughtful work is a sweet spot. It must launch from that sweet spot between just enough structure and just enough freedom. In specific terms, then what?

In the rigorous classroom, thoughtful work refers to learning tasks that have a teacher-facilitated focus yet leave enough room for student expression, originality, creativity, discovery, and accountability as they work toward a specific learning goal. Perhaps it's easier to think of the specifics of this abstract topic in terms of something we've grown comfortable with: curiosity. When intentionally designing a thoughtful task or planning opportunities for students to determine their own thoughtful tasks, teachers should ask themselves (or their students where appropriate): Will this task ultimately drive epistemic curiosity, or will it only get to diversive curiosity? If the answer is diversive, the task lacks rigor.

Once it's evident that a task will support epistemic curiosity, there are other hallmarks of rigorous and thoughtful tasks to check off your list. Thoughtful work in the well-developed classroom is not so specific that there are no opportunities for children to follow the questions or ideas that come up as they move through the task. It doesn't limit students in their means to pursue information, and it ideally lends itself to multiple ways to find information. Nor is it so open-ended that students struggle to know where to begin. It's up to teachers to ensure that thoughtful work strikes a delicate balance. Research or conversation has to be focused just enough to leave room for organic discovery.

As a function of scaffolding, tasks sometimes benefit learners most when the teacher determines them. To maintain rigor in the classroom when assigning specific work, we have to take care to ensure that the hallmarks of rigorous, thoughtful work remain in place. Yet in the well-developed classroom, students often have the chance to come up with their own work tasks. When students have the freedom to self-direct and decide how they want to approach deeper learning, it allows them to choose a task that best represents their own thinking or preferred learning style. This opens the door for the learning to become more relevant to them, which, as we know, makes rigor possible.

Thoughtful work is both a function of and a foundation for high-level questioning and academic discussion. Let me explain.

When pre-planned, well-developed, and rigorous high-level questioning and academic discussion are taking place in a classroom, they often work together to lead naturally to an authentic learning task. At some point, with thoughtful questions and engaging discussion stoking that epistemic curiosity, the class will hit a point where collectively, more information is needed to jump to the next rung of rigorous thought. Typically, this looks like a lull in or a flat-lining of a conversation. Students grow silent; an indicator of rigorous thinking beginning to wane. As teachers, our antennas for conversational plateaus must be up so we can sense when it's time to intervene and help students discover the information they need to restore lively discussion.

What's key in these moments of information gaps and conversational plateaus is that the teacher allows for breaks in discussion for an authentic, thoughtful learning task to close the information gap. When these moments come about organically, they will be most impactful if the teacher has a toolbox of prompts or mini-learning goals to provide just enough structure for successful, student-driven learning tasks.

However, in certain instances, like if the content is somewhat inhibiting or a learning goal requires a certain direction, thoughtful work will need to be planned in advance. In the well-developed classroom, the teacher plans for natural breaks in the discussion to prompt students to do some research or complete a task. After any task is complete, there's an inherent opportunity for high-level follow-up questions and a renewed, more elevated academic discussion, enhanced by the information and knowledge that all students just gained. Thoughtful tasks can be both a catalyst for and result of high-level questioning and rigorous discussion.

In any rigorous learning task, particularly those determined and driven by students, self-reflection is key. In the well-developed classroom, the teacher should guide a few, brief formative assessments so students can evaluate if their task is helping them advance toward the learning goal. If not, students should be supported as they adapt and improve their approach. The need to adapt is by no means a failure. In fact, adapting should be encouraged and recognized as a natural part of the discovery process as we follow our epistemic curiosity on the journey it wants to take us.

It's in the discovery process that students are exposed to more ideas, more concepts, more areas of study, more facts, more knowledge. The broader exposure students can get to all that can be learned, the more likely they will eventually stumble upon that thing that might just be the thing upon which they want to build a career.

Chapter Three

Imagination: Why Relevance Matters

Imagination is more important than knowledge. Knowledge is limited. Imagination encircles the world. —Albert Einstein

Imagination: Perfectly Ordinary

Scenario 1: A young orphan comes to learn he's a wizard with mystical powers living amongst ordinary people called Muggles. He is invited to the Hogwarts School of Witchcraft and Wizardry to learn, in secretive surroundings secluded from Muggles, how to perfect his wizarding skills. He befriends fellow classmates all the while confronting both the mundane and magical trappings of teendom: angst, social drama, school stress, romance, and, not least of all, a dark wizard by the name of Lord Voldemort who vows to conquer the wizarding world and subjugate all Muggles.

Scenario 2: A middle school student writing about what he thinks it might be like to grow up and be a fireman. Or a teacher. Or a real estate developer.

What's the difference between these scenarios? You might be thinking: what's not different? In specifics, much is different, of course. But at the core? Not much. At the core, both of these scenarios are nothing more than the workings of imagination.

The trouble is that we've projected a lot onto imagination that isn't there. We think of it as something reserved and to artists or writers of science fiction or fantasy. Sure, we believe that some people, those like Steve Jobs, appear to have rare and brilliant imaginations. In these cases, we put imagination on a pedestal and think of it as something most of us just do not and will never have. Or we think of it as something that runs wild in kids and then is necessarily tamed by facts and figures so that it can be channeled into the practical and productive. In adults, imagination is for the daydreamers, the time-wasters, the distracted. But us? We have work to get done and no time to let our imaginations run.

When did imagination become this thing that is either reserved for a brilliant few or something better left to toddlers at play? Because really, imagination is merely creating an image in your mind. J. K. Rowling sitting down to write her books? Creating images in her mind and putting written words to them. That middle school student writing about what being a teacher might be like? Creating images in his mind and putting written words to them. Imagination is rather ordinary. And we all use it all the time.

Merriam-Webster defines *imagine* as "to form a mental image (of something not present); to form a notion without sufficient basis." That's it. There's nothing about it being reserved for this group of people because they're young and it's appropriate, or for that group of people because they're geniuses and lucky. There's nothing about it being fit for art and not fit for science. And nothing about how it's this rarefied event that only precedes some stroke of insight. It's just creating an image in one's mind of something not directly or literally in front of one's eyes. That's all, folks.

In fact, make a point to notice how many times you use your imagination in the next few days. Leaving 15 minutes later than you'd planned and picturing all the traffic you're now certain you'll face? That's your imagination at work. Planning a classroom exercise and considering how your students might react? Imagination in use. Reading a book about the Civil War and visualizing a scene? Again, imagination. Working with a friend through a few options she might have to deal with a challenging coworker situation? You guessed it: imagination. Listening to a family member describe his pain after a surgical procedure and extending your empathy? Yep, you're trying to imagine what this experience has been like for him. Dreaming about the day you finally publish that book you've always wanted to write? You know the answer.

We use our imaginations all the time. We use imagination to attempt to stand in someone else's shoes, or step back in time to understand something from the past, or step forward in time to make future plans. Imagination is the tool we apply to fill in experience gaps; we just don't think of this as putting our imaginations to work. Imagination is how we bridge ourselves from where we are at this very moment to someplace else, any place a situation demands we go.

Students use imagination to open up their relatively small worlds. If imagination is how we fill experience gaps, it's especially critical for students at all levels of learning. Imagination is the bridge out of what they immediately know and into everything else.

Let's go back to our seventh-grader at the party confronted with alcohol. The child who's developed a habit of curiosity will naturally begin asking questions and, hopefully, come to conclusions that will help him avoid trouble. What happens if I take this sip of alcohol? What happens if my parents find out? Or if the police show up? What happens if my school finds out? What happens if I end up in the car with someone who's been drinking? But to have any impact, these questions need answers.

Curiosity is just part of the story. Imagination is another part.

What Is Academic Relevance?

It is a happy talent to know how to play. —Ralph Waldo Emerson

Relevance is the application of rigor, or the action taken with knowledge. At the far left end of the relevance (horizontal) axis, also called the action continuum, learners simply acquire knowledge. As they move along the action continuum, they apply it in increasingly complex ways, from one discipline, to multiple disciplines, to real-world predictable situations, and finally, to real-world unpredictable situations.

Rigor/Relevance Framework®

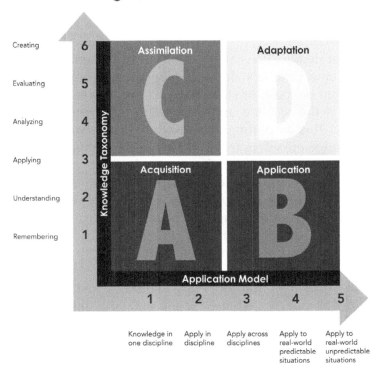

A	B	C	D
Students gather and store bits of knowledge and information. Students are primarily expected to remember or understand this knowledge.	Students use acquired knowledge to solve problems, design solutions, and complete work. The highest level of application is to apply knowledge to new and unpredictable situations.	Students extend and refine their acquired knowledge to be able to use that knowledge automatically and routinely to analyze and solve problems and create solutions.	Students think in complex ways and can apply their knowledge and skills. Even when confronted with perplexing unknowns, students can create solutions and take action that further develops their skills and knowledge.

As application advances, the use of knowledge becomes more relevant. Another way to think about this is that as a student travels along the action continuum, the possibilities open up. What a student can do with information becomes more dynamic, and thus what that student can do expands in possibility. Options grow.

For a simplified example, let's put ourselves in a ninth-grade math classroom. The teacher is explaining statistical probability. She guides her students in a lesson about the odds of getting heads or tails on the first flip of a coin, and then how the first outcome impacts the outcome odds for each subsequent flip. Aware that the biology teacher is currently covering what dictates gender determination in offspring, the math teacher asks her students to think about where probability can be found in other subjects. With just that one question, these students have been asked to increase the relevance of their knowledge. Students have no longer acquired basic understanding of probability for the mere sake of acquiring it. They now have a little something to *do* with that knowledge.

After a brief conversation about probability in biology, the teacher asks the students to imagine other instances where they've seen probability in their lives. "In a coin toss before a football game," one student says. "When trying to guess if my parents will make spaghetti or chicken, again, for dinner tonight," another says. "When trying to figure out what kinds of comments are more likely to be liked on Facebook," yet another shares. Now, the students are taking the knowledge they've gathered and using their imaginations to run through other scenarios, not necessarily in the confines of the classroom, where it might apply. They're using their imaginations to complete a mental image of something not in front of them. And as they do this more broadly, their use of that knowledge progresses to the next marker on the relevance axis.

Now the teacher asks if they can think of a scenario beyond their own lives where probability might be important. Let's imagine that these kids are in Florida and know a thing or two about hurricanes. After encouraging a five-second wait time to let students think and use their imaginations, the teacher invites responses. "Storm prediction," a student says. With a break in the discussion pre-planned, the teacher then asks the students to gather briefly in groups to dialogue over the implications of predicting the probability of a hurricane and how it might dictate the public's and the government's responses to it.

The students huddle and then share their points with the class. "If odds are low that a storm will hit," one group says, "then it will be fine for people to continue to go to work and to school." "If they can predict that the storm will be really strong, then the mayor will make sure that roads are closed and tell everyone not to drive or go anywhere," another group suggests. "Depending how bad the weather forecasters think the storm will be, they will tell everyone to board up their windows," the third group says.

With this, students have advanced yet again along the action continuum and are applying their knowledge about probability to real-world situations. They're not only imagining when probability might be used in the real world, they're also imagining the implications of different outcomes. The knowledge has moved from knowledge gathered just to say you know it, to action being taken with that knowledge in order to grasp its use in the real world. Facts and figures have been lifted off the page and into the imagination to bridge students to relevance.

Action Continuum

Acquisition of Knowledge ➡ Application of Knowledge

If curiosity is the conduit to rigor, then imagination is the conduit to relevance. In terms of relevance, I find it helpful to think of imagination as a bridge. If the movement from diversive curiosity to epistemic curiosity is what drives students up the rigor axis, then the length of the bridge is what pushes them along the relevance continuum. To apply knowledge to another class subject is to ask students to build a short imagination bridge to cross-disciplinary application. To ask students to apply knowledge to an unpredictable real-world situation is to ask them to build a much longer imagination bridge. To construct this bridge, they will have to fill in more experience gaps, which demands more curiosity, which in turn demands greater use of imagination.

But imagination plays more than just a behind-the-scenes role in the relevant classroom. It's not just the silent thought action students take when applying knowledge. In my experience, imagination as a learning application tool works best and, importantly, has the longest-lasting impact on students when it's used explicitly.

I would encourage you to deliberately engage with your students about what imagination is, how we use it, and how they're using it, even when they don't notice it. Tell them explicitly that when the wheels of their brains are spinning, and images are getting created and conjured to apply knowledge to multiple scenarios, their imaginations are bridging them to their relevant destination. Use the word and use it often. I've seen this have two effects: (1) demystifying imagination and (2) establishing a lifelong habit of it.

Just as we're born with a natural curiosity that we get socialized out of, we're born with a natural imagination that we also get socialized out of. At a certain age, inevitably one student will chastise another who still has an imaginary friend. These subtle social cues will slowly cause kids to think of boundless, fanciful, imaginative play as something that needs to be outgrown or contained. Playing teacher or army ranger will be traded in for playing video games. Imagination, which once ran like water from a wide-open spout, will slowly be turned off. When this happens, it gets rusty and all too often forgotten. Eventually, too many students begin to think they don't have "very good" imaginations and they start to believe the false idea that imagination is for the art kids and the Steve Jobses or the J. K. Rowlings of the world. We know this isn't true. So we must help prevent our students from believing it.

Curiosity is just part of the story. Imagination is another part.

Recall how epistemic curiosity naturally causes us to bump up against things we don't know, which causes us to want to know more? The virtuous cycle of gaining more and more knowledge is underway. But then what? If curiosity produces a bunch of knowledge ingredients, then imagination is what mixes them together to create something of a new form or effect. Individual ingredients become cake.

Imagination is the action of curiosity. Only recently have we discovered where imagination occurs in the brain: in a "widespread network of neurons (what [Dartmouth researchers] call the 'mental workspace') that consciously alters and manipulates images, symbols, and ideas, and gives us the intense mental focus that we need to come up with new ideas and solutions to complex problems" (Gregoire, 2013). The act of imagining is literally pulling from multiple parts of the brain. It is the active connection of disparate dots to result in something new. "When asked what his scientific thought process looked like," said Alex Schlegel, one of the Dartmouth researchers, "Einstein would say that he'd take an image in his mind and play around with it and manipulate it, looking at it from different angles—combining and breaking things apart" (Gregoire, 2013).

Einstein is the perfect person to bring up to emphasize imagination's power in learning and creating. Thought experiments have long been a common tool in physics, philosophy, and other areas of study. But Einstein, perhaps more than anyone else, mainstreamed the idea of thought experiments. He very famously changed the world when he wondered what would happen if he were to travel at the speed of light. Shorthand answer: It was his decades-long, rigorous pursuit of an answer to this question that would lead to the theory of relativity ($E=mc^2$), the creation of the atomic bomb, and many other game-changing discoveries.)

Einstein famously loved thought experiments (Brown and Fehige, 2016), which can be broadly defined as "devices of the imagination used to investigate the nature of things." When the crevasse between what he knew and what he ultimately wanted to know was so broad, thought experiments provided a stepping-stone strategy to incrementally progress. His imagination would help unearth a knowledge gap, which would guide the next line of inquisition, and so on and so forth. Thought experiments provided frameworks under which he could think about things he didn't fully understand. They would bridge him from where he was to where he wanted to go. By tossing around bits of knowledge, looking at them in different ways, imagining how they might come together in this scenario or that, Einstein would break through to new solutions and ideas.

Imagination is the key that unlocks creativity and originality. It lets knowledge loose to merge and form into ideas.

No, we do not have to create classrooms of mini-Einsteins. That's the risk of using him as an example. He is high on a pedestal, and rightfully so. But that he used imagination to solve problems and create new and original thoughts was perfectly ordinary.

As teachers, it is our charge to nurture college- and career-ready students. To do this, we need to normalize imagination in the classroom. We need to bang the drum that imagination is something we all have and all use—*daily*. It's up to us pre-school and elementary teachers to help maintain students' natural predilection for creating characters or partaking in imaginative play when we begin to see it wane. It's up to us to help them evolve that innate tendency into something more relevant to their maturation and changing curiosities. From there, it's up to us middle school teachers to sustain students' imaginations and encourage them to apply what they're learning to other classes and their expanding interests. It's up to us high school teachers to guide students in imagining how their academic interests might evolve and unfold in college, or translate into jobs and what that specific work might look like and require. It's up to us teachers to help students avoid losing their natural-born tendency to let their imaginations run wild. It's up to us to help them create a habit of relying on their imaginations to bridge them out of the limits of their knowledge and experiences. It's up to us to help them keep their powers of imagination honed and ready so that when they confront big problems or roadblocks—in life, in careers—they have the tools to imagine their way into the best solutions.

An important note on bridging students to career relevance: we must bear in mind that our students are a function of their life experiences. After all, that is why young children begin using imagination in the first place—to try to figure out what the world beyond their little lives might be. Many of our students are not exposed to a broad range of career options; they know what their parents do for work and perhaps some of their friends' parents. But beyond that, we must consider that career awareness for some students might end there. It's up to us specifically to cite and name careers and jobs across a spectrum. When it comes to career readiness, not only are we preparing our students with the skills needed for high-level jobs, we're also introducing them to what those high-level jobs *could be*.

Recall how George Washington Carver's art teacher dared him to imagine a different career path with those images of plant life he so loved to paint? And Carver took that call. No apparent limiting belief stood in his way. Ostensibly, he could imagine a future in botany enough to go create it. By normalizing imagination and habitually discussing it in the classroom, we can prove to students they do in fact have active, ready-to-get-to-work, healthy imaginations. We can help them remove the limiting belief that they're not qualified for this task, or they won't add much value to that project, or they will never be able to get that job because it requires too much creativity and imagination. Instead, we'll help students develop and maintain a confidence in their ability to imagine their way to new ideas and solutions.

Merge a habit of epistemic curiosity with a habit of imagination and you've got a Quad D classroom, outfitting students with a Quad D attitude, and preparing them for a Quad D life. Let's now imagine the three indicators of intentional relevance in your Quad D classroom.

Relevance Indicator: Meaningful Work

A wall turned sideways is a bridge. —Angela Davis

I like nonsense; it wakes up the brain cells. —Dr. Seuss

In his book *On Writing*, Stephen King devotes the first portion to vignettes about his childhood. He looks back at notable experiences from his life to piece together those that shaped his career as a writer. As a first-grader, King got chronic ear and throat infections so severe that he repeatedly missed school—so much school that it was decided he'd be pulled out and restart first grade the following fall. All of a sudden, young King had lots of time on his hands. Without a television in his house, he "read his way through approximately six tons of comic books, progressed to Tom Swift and Dave Dawson . . . then moved on to Jack London's bloodcurdling animal tales." Eventually, he began writing his own stories. "Imitation preceded creation," King observed. He would copy stories verbatim but add some of his own descriptions here and there (King, 2010).

At one point, he showed one of his "copycat hybrid" creations to his mom, and something life-altering happened: she smiled (King, 2010). She was impressed and proud. She asked King if he'd come up with the story himself, to which he had to admit he hadn't. Deflated, King studied his mom's face, sensing disappointment. But then she said to him, "Write one of your own, Stevie . . . I bet you could do better" (King, 2010). The rest is horror history.

Permission and encouragement are critical to supporting imagination. Fear and self-doubt stymie imagination. Surely this is something you've experienced yourself and perhaps still do. There's great trepidation in sharing our ideas. They feel so personal, so raw. So if people don't approve of them, it feels almost like they don't approve of us.

How can we as teachers keep our classrooms as safe zones of imagination? Just as we must steadfastly remind our students that questions are linchpins of learning and not indicators of ignorance, we must steadfastly remind them that imaginations are messy and are meant to be. If they weren't, Einstein would have solved his "what happens if I move as fast as the speed of light?" thought experiment much more quickly. Imagination bridges are not always straight or swift.

Imagination, that "mental workspace" as the Dartmouth researchers called it, is inherently a neutral zone—neither good nor bad, neither right nor wrong. It is allowed to be, *supposed* to be wild and without order. It is supposed to yield a range of ideas. Imagination is a numbers game: the more ideas it produces, the more likely it will produce that one idea that sticks. And the more fodder you feed an imagination—the more knowledge and information bits, the more ingredients—the more the odds of that numbers game improve.

How do we remove the fear from using our imaginations? Make it playful. Make it meaningful and memorable. Make it fun. Imagination should be fun like it was when we were kids. It's gotten so serious. Remind your students to have fun when using their imaginations and encourage them to avoid the trap of believing imagination is serious or rarefied. Imaginations, those judgment-free zones, cannot be graded. By equating imagination with play, we can help condition students to approach imagination-driven work with the same relaxation they apply to actual playtime. It wouldn't hurt for us teachers to model this by tossing out some of our own silly ideas to students now and then.

If thoughtful work is the intentionally designed sweet spot between just enough structure and just enough freedom, then meaningful work is that which permits and empowers imagination to lead students toward multiple destinations of relevance. Put another way, thoughtful work is the launching pad to rigor, and meaningful work is the relevant destination. It's work that leaves room for students to build imagination bridges to places of relevance that both resonate with the learners and strengthen their capacity to connect knowledge dots and arrive someplace new. It also allows students to convey and express those destinations in the way—through the medium, tool, or product—that feels most natural.

The teacher's role in this exercise in creation and originality is to support and guide students over the bridges they construct. We do this by encouraging students to be playful with their knowledge, to tinker with it, to toss it around in that messy "mental workspace" of imagination. We permit them to share ideas that might seem nonsensical by reminding them that a nonsensical idea might be the one that triggers the new idea that catches hold.

What does the creation of meaningful work look like, in more tangible terms, in the well-developed classroom? In the rigor section, we discussed that when designing an intentionally thoughtful work task for students, teachers should ask themselves if the task will stoke epistemic curiosity. If the answer is yes, then the task is rigorous. Similarly, when designing an intentionally meaningful work task, teachers should ask themselves *How long of an imagination bridge will students need to build to complete this task?* If the answer is "short"—i.e., the bridge will only need to get them from my English class over to their civics class—then the task is low on the relevance action continuum. If the answer is "long"—i.e., the bridge will need to transport them off their school campus and into, for example, the judicial branch of the government—then the task is more advanced on the action continuum. If the task allows for multiple possible bridges to take students to multiple destinations of relevance—e.g., a task that requires students to consider where in the real world creating evidence-based arguments might be important—then we're at the far end of the continuum.

Explaining and modeling this process to crafting meaningful work—thinking through imagination bridge length—to your students is also a hallmark of a well-developed classroom. After all, as King noted, imitation precedes creation. Once your students observe you distinguishing plain old busy work from meaningful work, they can go on to create their own meaningful work tasks, which naturally demands the most rigorous levels of thinking. Again, we find ourselves in Quad D.

As students build their relevant imagination bridges, our job is to remind them to think critically and dig deeper. Have they considered it from this angle, or that other angle? Have they let their imaginations get sufficiently messy? Have they tossed around enough knowledge ingredients to see if they can make a new idea cake? As our students complete meaningful work or come up with their own original meaningful task, we take care to guide their imaginations outside of the walls of the classroom and into the working worlds they will one day inhabit.

Relevance Indicator: Authentic Resources

Research is to see what everybody else has seen, and to think what nobody else has thought. —Albert Szent-Gyorgyi

Authentic resources: their importance in the classroom is often overlooked. But the good news is that this indicator of relevance is quite straightforward. The goal of authentic resources is simple: help students learn how to use real resources efficiently as one would at a real-world job.

News reporters operate under tight deadlines. They must report on a story before it's, well, old news. This means that to be effective at their jobs, they have to know where they will be most likely to find the information they need and how to navigate those resources efficiently. It's a real skill, one that's required in the many jobs that have a research component.

Let's say a reporting team is writing a news story about a series of retail store closings in a town. They will need to learn why this is happening and how it's impacting nearby business owners and residents. A logical place for them to start would be by conducting an interview with someone whose business recently closed. This primary source will provide insights that will prompt the team to research things such as retail rental rates, spending habits of local residents, changing demographics, and so on. They'll discover some things during research that will then cause them to want to find other information or interview other subjects. Eventually, through a mix of primary and secondary sources and qualitative and quantitative data, the team will be able to paint an evidence-backed picture of why so many stores in town are closing.

This is what researching a topic or question looks like in the real world: it's iterative, it unfolds, and it has twists and turns. It's broadly goal-oriented, directed and logical, but still allowed to take shape organically and leave room for unexpected discoveries. The researcher must remain flexible and know when to consult a new resource, primary or secondary, and when to move on from resources that aren't proving relevant.

These are the skills we're aiming to develop and condition in our students. There are two components to this:

1. helping students think strategically through which resources are most logical for a given task, and
2. helping students learn to mine resources efficiently for information.

To do this, we must intentionally design research-driven opportunities with these components in mind. For the learning to be relevant, we want our research to replicate that same mix of directed and organic seen in real-world jobs like that of our news reporters. Our goal is to strike a balance between giving students structure and leaving room for them to learn by trial and error. Meaning, when assigning a research project, we can't leave students with a topic so open-ended that they are just spinning their wheels. This amounts to frustration and no skill development. The research must be pinned to an essential problem or question. In the well-developed classroom, this problem or question must also be one that can be pursued and probed via multiple and multi-format resources. The universe of available resources should be reasonably and realistically, but not totally, limited. We should stop short of telling students which resources to use and when. Only by doing will students learn.

It's our job then to coach students as they set out to consider what they need to know and which resources will most likely get them to that information. While we don't want to tell them specifically where to begin, we can engage in a conversation about imagining the merits of beginning with this resource or that one, or imagining why a primary resource may or may not be a useful place to start.

When we sense a student is stumped or chasing a cold trail, we can help by discussing with them tips and tricks to spot the relevant information. Perhaps there are key words they can look out for, or another Google search to try. Maybe the questions they're asking an interview subject are too vague and there are ways to word them to be more closely related to the research goal.

All in all, we want to take care to avoid direct commands, and instead provide clues as students embark on their research hunt. After all, we're trying to help students gain and develop the skills to be able to, one day, conduct research independently at work without needing someone else's help. We're trying to help them learn how to use a broad suite of resources and tools to solve problems, find solutions to complex issues, support arguments, and complete tasks. The more realistic we can make these classroom exercises, the less our students will come to need us.

A quick but important note: any use of internet research must be preceded by a conversation about discerning authentic from fake resources online. By habituating students to ask questions about how to identify trustworthy sources of information online, they will learn how to do it themselves and, eventually, reflexively so.

Relevance Indicator: Learning Connections

Logic will get you from A to B. Imagination will take you everywhere. —Albert Einstein

When your classroom is consistently relevant, you will notice something magical begin to happen. You will no longer need to prompt your students, in subtle or overt ways, to connect the content at hand to experiences from their own lives or the outside world. Making connections becomes a habit. And this is the ultimate goal.

By taking care to create and let students create meaningful tasks, by allowing students to interact with and explore authentic resources in a way that mirrors their use in the working world, you are well on your way to cultivating students who habitually connect dots. But there's something you can do to ensure this becomes an achieved goal for every student in your classroom.

Journalist Charles Duhigg's wife commented on the weight he'd put on recently. Then she commented again. And again. And again. Until finally Duhigg decided it was time to admit that his chocolate-chip-cookie-a-day habit was showing up on his waistline. He realized it was time to break the habit. To do this, he recognized a knowledge gap that needed to be filled: how are habits formed in the first place? He figured if he could learn this, he could reverse engineer it to un-form his cookie habit (Duhigg, 2014).

A natural reporter, Duhigg began digging. What he discovered is that all habits operate within the same habit loop: cue, routine, reward, repeat. He began observing his cookie habit, tested a few different twists on it, and eventually realized that for him, the cue was a specific moment in the afternoon while at the office. This would trigger his routine—the habit itself—of traveling up to the cafeteria to buy a cookie. Then he would munch his cookie while chatting with friends. The reward for him, he determined, was the fun, social break he got from work. Once he had this aha moment, he was able to replace the cookie habit with a daily and zero-calorie afternoon gab session with friends (Duhigg, 2014).

Why not explicitly aim to make a learning connections habit in your classroom?

First, you'll want to define the habit you and all your students are striving to form: a habit of linking what they're learning to life outside school. Make a classroom commitment to learning connections. Then, perhaps, together come up with some sort of habit loop that will help motivate your students to develop a linking thinking routine.

What cue can you come up with that will trigger students to quietly pause and call on their imaginations to create a bridge from the content at hand to some sort of relevant destination outside school? Maybe it's hanging a poster of a bridge on the wall, and perhaps in the early stages of routine building, you point to it throughout a class session to remind students it's time to make a learning connection. Perhaps you devote a class session to having your students build a bridge out of popsicle sticks to serve as a sort of classroom mascot. Whatever the cue, let your students know that you'll be pointing to the cue at least once every session to remind them to do some linking thinking.

As a class, what reward can you come up with that will be meaningful to your students? Maybe it's some sort of points program, and as students share a learning connection they made with the class, they get a point. Those who've accrued the most points at the end of a semester might win something. Or perhaps it's a known expectation that at the end of each class, you'll ask for a volunteer to share a learning connection and reward them with a get-out-of-homework card good for one use. Whatever it is, the reward has to have value to your students.

If we want our students to develop a habit of making learning connections, we have to make the formation of this habit fun for them. Be playful and imaginative, and involve them in devising the process.

But perhaps most important is explaining to students why the ability to make learning connections is so valuable to their academic and professional lives.

Are you one of the millions who have watched Steve Jobs' viral 2005 Stanford commencement address? If not, please pause now and find it on YouTube. It will surely inspire.

In his address, Jobs discusses that when it comes to how our lives unfold, we often only see how the dots got connected in the rearview mirror. He was referring to the many ways he connected disparate dots to form entirely new concepts and ideas over the course of his career. But during his collection of those dots, he didn't yet know how or when or to what he'd connect them. As an example, he shared that after he dropped out of college, he continued to couch surf in dorms so he could drop in on various classes. He followed his curiosity into all sorts of courses, including a calligraphy class. In it, he learned about the art behind typefaces, about what makes typography aesthetic, about how to proportionally space various fonts to be most appealing. Through this course, Jobs gained an appreciation for the subtle components of creating beautiful fonts, all the while believing it was knowledge gained for nothing more than pleasure (Jobs, 2005).

Ten years later when he and his team of computer engineers were building the first Macintosh computer, the knowledge of typefaces that had been swirling around in his brain found its destined landing place. In a move that was revolutionary, Jobs and company built the first personal computer that incorporated a large number of pleasing fonts. Macs were the first computers to appeal to people who wanted form as well as function (Jobs, 2005).

Steve Jobs followed his curiosity into a class. Years later, he connected it to another discipline—and changed the world.

Connecting dots is how we break new ground, however big or small. By explaining that learning connections are the way we can build imagination bridges to not-yet-discovered destinations, we can impress upon our students that the rewards of a habit of making learning connections can far exceed that which we can offer in the classroom.

Inspiring our students to forge learning connections is how we prevent meaningful work from stalling in Quad B and instead propel it into Quad D—and beyond to who knows where.

Chapter Four

Agency: Why Learner Engagement Matters

This old notion of swallowing down other people's ideas and problems just as they have worked them out, without putting our brain and originality into it and making them applicable to our specific needs must go. And the sooner we let them go, the sooner we will be a free and independent people.
—George Washington Carver

The Electrified, Energized, Engaged Classroom

You know immediately when you walk into a classroom where the students are engaged in rigorous and relevant learning. You can sense it. It's an energy, a spirit, a synchronicity. There's a vitality and electricity to these classrooms that you can just *feel*.

A teacher can get all of her rigorous and relevant ducks in a row. She can have all sorts of techniques lined up that stoke curiosity up the rigor scale. Instructional design to bridge imaginations across the relevance continuum can be at the ready. But if there is no intentional plan to engage students, all this effort will be for naught. If there is no strategically designed environment in place to bring rigor and relevance to life in the classroom, students will not engage. It is the students who are engaged in their learning—active agents in their cognitive and social development—who will be prepared for careers and life in the twenty-first century.

We hear this a lot, that it is our responsibility and goal as educators to prepare students for life in the twenty-first century. But what does this mean beyond the fact that we're no longer in the twentieth century?

In his book *Drive*, Daniel Pink puts it this way. He explains how twentieth-century careers generally required compliance. Most jobs, even high-paying, high-skill ones, were mechanical in nature. They were routine, rule-based, and of narrow focus. They solved relatively simple problems that often had only one solution. In the twenty-first century, many of these jobs have been automated or outsourced. The high-skill careers that have taken their place are more complex and demand greater cognition; they have to be in order to outperform the average computer. Furthermore, the problems we face today are far more conceptual, interdisciplinary, and multifaceted. And we're seeing more jobs where employees regularly have to work remotely with people in other cultures (Davies, Fidler, & Gorbis, 2011). These days, rarely do we operate under a clear set of rules, and rarely are we attempting to solve just one problem or problems with just one solution (Pink, 2011).

Consider the issues we as educators are grappling with. We're grappling with how to overhaul an entire system that was built in and for a twentieth-century world. We're struggling with what to change and how to change it so that we can better prepare students for the lives and careers they will face upon graduation in this century. We're questioning curriculum, content, classroom design, evaluation and assessment procedures, leadership structure, and policy. We're trying to figure out how to teach inclusively to an increasingly diverse student set—meeting a broad set of learner needs while still being able to operate efficiently and cover required material. The issues are many, the solutions are unclear, the consequences are real and human. There is nothing rote or mechanical about what we educators are trying to solve.

Rigorous and relevant instructional design tees up students for learning that will advance their cognitive abilities and capacity. Rigor and relevance provide the framework for students to learn how to deal with complex, ambiguous problems that present many possible outcomes. But students will only milk rigor and relevance for their worth if they *engage* with it.

If curiosity drives rigor, and imagination drives relevance, what drives engagement? The answer is *agency*.

For twentieth-century careers, it was sufficient for students to learn rules and perform routine, repetitive tasks. It was enough for the teacher to stand at the front of the classroom and lecture while students took notes and then solved straightforward problems. Last century, the teacher-driven classroom with relatively passive students generally mirrored the working world where careers tended to be siloed in one discipline.

Not true anymore. If we are going to prepare our students for the world they will have to navigate, then we need to mirror that world in our classrooms. This means designing a learner environment that supports and inspires agency in every student. We must invite students to be active agents in their cognitive and social growth. It is only when students are proactively participating in their own learning that they are engaged. And it is only through engagement that they can hone the facets of agency that will enable their success in twenty-first century careers.

Let's return one last time to our seventh grader at the party who is offered alcohol. He's a student of rigor and relevance, so his curiosity has been well nurtured; he knows immediately to run through probing questions to examine the situation. His imagination is active and reflexive; he knows to consider many possible outcomes of the many possible choices he could make in this moment. But then what?

From there, the child must have the wherewithal, the confidence, and the awareness of choice in using his voice to take informed action. He must be an active participant in his decisions, as opposed to being at the whim or mercy of others, or, perhaps worse, unaware he has choice and voice at all. The ability to consider multiple angles, multiple possible results from multiple possible paths, choose the most suitable informed solution, and act on that preference—that is the breadth of possibility that agency affords. That is what active engagement in the direction of one's life looks like.

Curiosity and imagination are parts of the story. Agency is the final part.

What Is Academic Engagement?

My mission in life is not merely to survive, but to thrive; and to do so with some passion, some compassion, some humor, and some style. —Maya Angelou

What does one need to be truly effective at one's job today—in this complicated world, where the list of stakeholders only seems to grow, the inputs on what we can and have to do only expand, the stakes of our decisions only get higher, and where we regularly have to adapt to new technologies?

To excel in careers today, one needs the following characteristics:

- self-awareness and self-reflection
- self-respect
- confidence and humility
- self-direction and accountability
- resilience and flexibility
- choice and voice

When these traits are in place, the person is empowered to take informed action. In other words, the person has agency.

I like to call these traits the facets of agency. From my years in the classroom and coaching educators in the quest to increase rigor, relevance, and engagement, I've observed that these facets must be nurtured in the classroom if we are to help students find and exercise their agency. Fortunately, by intentionally bringing engagement to our instruction, we can ensure all facets of agency are inspired and activated in our students. It is helpful first to define these facets as they pertain to student agency and engagement and consider their long-term implications and benefits.

Self-Awareness and Self-Reflection. To me, these two facets of agency go hand in hand. If one is self-aware, one is self-reflecting. If one is self-reflecting, one is self-aware. Together, they are the enablers of personal growth. It is only by exploring who we are, where we are, and why we are that we can determine how to become who we want to be. To be self-reflective and self-aware is to be fearlessly honest with ourselves and to take full accountability for our behaviors and actions. It is also to recognize that we hold the power to change our behaviors and actions; it is within the full potential of our agency to do so.

Self-Respect. Fearless self-awareness and self-reflection is the conduit to self-respect. Self-respect is the natural byproduct of liking and accepting ourselves for who we are, while remaining mindful that we have the power to enact change in our lives. Self-respect is recognizing our strengths and weaknesses and still being able to function productively in spite of our limits. It is also respecting our boundaries and the boundaries of others.

Confidence and Humility. With self-awareness and self-respect come confidence, but a version driven by humility, not arrogance. Agency is most effective when confidence is authentic and honest, or existing within the acceptance of our limits. This naturally puts our strengths into perspective and infuses our confidence with humility. From this quiet confidence, we can play to our strengths as we pursue goals, as well as celebrate the strengths of others and support them as they set out to achieve goals. We can also acknowledge others' limits without condescension.

Self-Direction and Accountability. With humble confidence, we trust ourselves to take initiative in advancing our learning, effort, growth, goals, careers—whatever we're working toward. We also take responsibility for our progress and our struggles and understand our agency in sustaining progress and persevering through struggles. Our reflex is not to place blame, but instead to look inward to self-reflect and determine what we can change and improve.

Resilience and Flexibility. We are aware that by definition acting with agency comes with some risk. Since we have humble confidence and acknowledge that we have limits, we recognize that failure is always a possibility, but this does not paralyze us. When we work with others, we recognize that they, too, are fallible. We see our failures and those of others not as final, but as feedback. We pick up, proceed where reasonable, and adapt to avoid hitting the same roadblocks.

Choice and Voice. We recognize that we have choice and take informed action as needed or appropriate. We confidently use our voice to express our dreams, fears, questions, boundaries, needs, interests, beliefs, self-doubts, and preferences. We see choice and voice as our natural tools of empowerment, and we apply them with respect for ourselves and for those around us.

All of these facets are both the inputs and outputs of agency. They feed our wherewithal to be productive agents in our lives, and also stem from it in a virtuous cycle.

Where to begin to support these facets of agency in our classrooms so that we can engage our students? The best place to start, in my experience, is with a mindset shift.

When thinking about what engagement means, I encourage you to rethink how you view the classroom. The classroom is not the place where students come to learn content. It's not the place where they come to get information from us in order to complete homework. It's not even just the place where they come to think more rigorously and relevantly. The *engaged* classroom is far more than just these things. It's a training ground. When setting forth to grasp and create an engaging classroom for learners, we need to think differently about what the classroom is. *The classroom is a training ground for success in careers and life.*

To make it so, we have to mirror the dynamics that require agency in our classrooms so that students are well fortified with agency when they confront these dynamics in the working world. We must intentionally design a classroom that enables and advances learner engagement. Play. Have fun. Make your classroom environment feel real. When this environment is in place, agency has full room to take root, grow, and blossom into a positive, productive condition for all of our students that they can then take into their lives beyond school.

When every one of our students is acting from a place of empowerment in our classroom, when each is actively engaged in his or her learning, then we have that electrified classroom. It's like we as teachers provide the outlet—we get all the wires of engagement in place, and the students plug in. Or they don't. They must act in order to do so. When they utilize their agency to this end, then we're in one of those classrooms where you can just *feel* the exuberant energy of engaged learners.

How do we line up all the necessary wires for engagement electricity? In addition to thinking of the classroom as training ground, we start with another sweeping change in our mindsets as educators: we rethink our sense of authority in the classroom. What's key in the engaged classroom is that utilization of agency. All too often, teachers thwart student agency. Doing so is at direct odds with engagement. If we want engaged learners—and we do—then we teachers have to take a step back. We must take our rightful role as shepherds, not commanders; as enablers, not generals; as facilitators, not didacts. We are the conduits to electricity; the students *are* the electricity—that is, if we get out of their way.

We do this for two primary reasons. First, this mirrors real-world dynamics in high-skill jobs. High-skill careers require even more self-direction from employees. When the nature of work grows more complex and interconnected, it's no longer possible or efficient for a leader or manager to be an expert in all inputs into a business or department. In the twenty-first century career landscape, individuals have to show more autonomy, expertise, initiative, authority, and agency to be effective in their roles. Rarely are projects or tasks explicitly handed down from on high anymore; doing so bogs down the process and reduces a company's agility and competitiveness (Balls, 2013). Instead, companies are empowering individuals to determine how to go about getting their work done. The management hierarchy in many companies is flattening, and in some, it has been removed entirely (Balls, 2013). In 2014, online shoe retailer Zappos famously removed all managers, stripping the company of traditional corporate hierarchy.

Second, we've talked about how we are born with curiosity and imagination, but then get socialized out of both. We are also born with a natural sense of agency, and we lose much of that in our youth, as well. This can happen for any number of reasons. Babies do what they want. They do what they can because they're exploring and it's exhilarating. They are curious and follow this curiosity straight to where it wants them to go, like right into the electrical socket. In such cases, we adults have to intervene for their safety. Adults will always need to intervene in the lives of children for their health and well-being. But intervention in the child's natural-born desire to self-direct (Pink, 2011) often takes on different forms throughout the child's developing years. Perhaps it's an overly strict caretaker, or a highly rigid teacher, or an excessively authoritarian parent.

To the child whose brain remains in active development and who is constantly navigating entirely new situations and emotions, distinguishing between when authority is necessary and in his or her best interests and when it's serving an adult's ulterior motives or preferences is difficult.

When a significant person in a child's life repeatedly blunts his or her budding agency, it can result in a confusion that can ultimately cause the child to develop unhealthy boundaries, for themselves and for others (Tartakovsky, 2014). Or the child in such circumstances could slowly lose his or her voice. He will begin to feel they don't have choice and, thus, develop patterns (Cherry, 2016) of merely taking orders or acting subserviently in certain scenarios. Or she might lose her ability to trust her gut and listen to what feels to be authentically who she is and instead morph into another's idea of what she should be. The child can also fail to develop a respect for others' boundaries, leading to delinquent behavior toward others (University of New Hampshire, 2012). In any such cases, children lose some or all of their agency.

I'm sure each of us, even the most confident and experienced among us, can look back on our careers and recall instances where we were afraid to speak up, defend our boundaries, fight for what we felt was fair. Or even more simply, we were scared to ask that question, or share that idea because we lacked full faith in our strengths in spite of our weaknesses. Many of us can also recall how much effort it took to break these patterns and regain our agency in our professional lives, even our personal lives. And perhaps some of us can also reflect back to our developing years and understand how we came to lose some of our agency.

Children, particularly younger kids, are naturally inclined to believe what adults tell them (Association for Psychological Science News, 2010); this is a function of adults perceived and real authority over them. If we are to support their agency, we must allow students to question what even we, the teachers, are saying. (Of course, part of our responsibility here is to coach students on how to respectfully challenge someone's line of thinking.) If our goal is to condition students to consume information with a critical and discerning eye, will we look credible if we simultaneously tell them what we say doesn't apply? Putting conditions on when students can follow their curiosity to clearer understanding will undermine our larger goal. The same goes for helping students use similar discernment with those who seek to assert some form of authority over them. Doing so will help train our students to be able to sense when someone is trying to take advantage of them.

Make no mistake: I am not calling for anarchy. The teacher in the engaged classroom is still ultimately in charge, and the students must know and respect this. Respect for one's self and for others is a huge part of agency. I'm simply saying that if there's any hope of creating an engaging learner environment where students are free to experiment with their budding agency and feel safe and supported doing so, the teacher must take a step back in her authority so that the students can take a step forward in their own agency. The two are mutually exclusive, inversely related: too much of one means too little of the other.

To achieve the engaged classroom is to achieve a delicate balance: between teacher authority and student freedom, and between environment structure and student direction. Striking this balance is challenging, but possible. To support your students' agency without losing control of the classroom or being overly directive, tell your students exactly *why* you're giving them the freedoms you're giving them and *how* they must learn to use them responsibly and to the benefit of both their individual development and the development of their peers. With your oversight, make *them* jointly accountable for achieving and maintaining this delicate balance. After all, inviting students to actively participate in the whys of the Rigor/Relevance Framework is how we engage them and show our respect for their inherent agency.

In the rigorous, relevant, *and* engaged classroom, the teacher is the conductor, orchestrating students to work individually and collaboratively to create harmonious, electrified music. We are coordinating and facilitating as the students glean experience in the training ground that is our engaged classroom, dress rehearsal for the real thing. As the conductor, we recognize that our students have an enormous amount to contribute to our classrooms and the world. We teachers—conductors, coaches, guides, shepherds, enablers, stewards— are here to support every last student in finding the agency to discover and share the full extent of his or her potential.

The three indicators of learner engagement are designed to help you pull off just that.

Learner Engagement Indicator: Active Participation

Tell me and I forget. Teach me and I remember. Involve me and I learn. —Chinese proverb as quoted by Benjamin Franklin

Being a teacher allows witnessing moments where human capacity for compassion, kindness, and creativity gets so beautifully displayed that these moments stay with us forever. One of those moments for me happened with my sixth-grade language arts class. While I planned each of my lessons with active participation in mind, in this particular year, I had a student—we'll call him Teddy—with cerebral palsy. Each day, he entered my classroom in a wheelchair with a special laptop where he could tap individual letters to generate a selection of full words from which he could choose his intended word. At first, I hesitated to press Teddy, not wanting to inadvertently make him feel self-conscious about his physical limitations. However, it was a known rule in my classroom that everyone was expected to participate actively. This rule would be rendered meaningless to the kids if I couldn't follow it myself. Teddy's presence meant that I had to identify alternative and multiple ways for students to communicate, perform, and engage as we learned new content.

That spring, each of my classes wrote, directed, and acted in one-act plays for their parents and peers. Along with the criteria for structure in the script and staging, I insisted that the production have an active role for every student in each class. That role could be in the writing, acting, or staging of the play.

Teddy's class chose to write a play about a tennis match, and without my interference or prompting, he and his classmates decided that he would play the role of the chair umpire, responsible for calling "fault" or "out," among other things. Teddy sat on the sidelines of the "court," turning his head slightly to the right and to the left while tracking the volley and mediating the match. He and his classmates, on their own, found a way to make Teddy an active player in the performance, rather than relegating him to a less visible role, like writing.

On the day of the production, Teddy's parents and both sets of grandparents filled the front row. Teddy beamed throughout the performance, and I confess to getting a little choked up. My students taught me what I needed to understand about active participation. I vowed in that moment never to view any students through any perceived limits and instead make it fact that every last child who passed through my doors would be actively involved in my classroom. My students showed me that there was great power in leaving how every last student would actively engage to their imaginative minds and entrusting them to make decisions. This trust emboldened them, it motivated them, and thus they felt a sense of accountability to themselves and each other. In my experience, when students are allowed to determine how they will participate, collaboration and compassion take over.

The driving force behind active participation is motivation. If students are to actively participate in class, they must find the pull to do so. When we were discussing the rigor Thoughtful Work rubric indicator, we referenced Daniel Pink's research about what motivates a modern-day employee. The carrot-and-stick approach fails to motivate those working under ambiguous circumstances where how a task should get completed and what it will look like in the end is not defined. To motivate people today, work, and those who might be overseeing it, must leave room for a person's natural desire for mastery, purpose, and autonomy (Pink 2011).

At the classroom and learner level, the Rigor/Relevance Framework naturally speaks to all three of these desires. Thoughtful Work promotes autonomy. Meaningful Work promotes a sense of purpose to an individual. Formative Processes and Tools, the third engagement indicator, support and ensure mastery. All the motivation ducks are lined up in a row. But then what? We must remind students that it is our job as teachers to ensure that the structure is in place for rigor, relevance, and engagement. But then it's *their* job to actually get in there and engage. To do this, we get the ducks in the row, and then get out of the way. Just as the manager seeking to motivate modern-day employees tells them the problem that needs solving, and then gets out of the way and lets them solve it.

By reminding students that they—not teachers, not content, not standards—are at the center of their learning, they naturally feel a sense of duty. They are motivated to participate, they are motivated to take responsibility, and they are motivated to improve. When I let my sixth graders come up with the idea for the play, write the script, assign the roles, and direct the performance, it was clear to them that they were the drivers of this task, not me or anything else. I put a loose structure in place and then handed them the reins. This sense of empowered responsibility motivated them not only to ensure their own participation, but everyone else's as well.

Thoughtful work says that we must resist the urge to assign tasks that are clearly defined or bound by just one subject or possible solution. Instead, we must look for and create opportunities for students to wrestle with interdisciplinary tasks that have multiple possible outcomes. Meaningful work says that we let students use their imaginations to work through those multiple possible outcomes, experimenting with applying their knowledge in different ways and to different scenarios. We support and guide them as they hone in on a solution and express it as they see fit.

All the while, we are keeping the focus in the classroom on those forces that keep students motivated to engage. We circulate, observe them as they work, and ensure they have the tools and resources they need to grapple with the task at hand. We remind students to exercise their agency when working through something, to make choices, take accountability for those choices, and adapt and seek improvements as needed to arrive at a successful completion. We keep the focus of the learning on *them* so that they maintain a focus on the responsibility for their learning with which we've entrusted them.

Learner Engagement Indicator: Learning Environment

> *I've missed more than 9,000 shots in my career. I've lost almost 300 games. Twenty-six times, I've been trusted to take the game winning shot and missed. I've failed over and over and over again in my life. And that is why I succeed.* —Michael Jordan

Michael Jordan embodies humble confidence by underscoring the important role that his failures have played in his success. This definition of success is not the one that seems to dominate the headlines these days, in this era of historical bonuses and billion-dollar tech companies that seem to crop up overnight.

Success in our culture is getting bigger, faster, and, it seems, less accessible. We repeatedly hear stories about precocious teenagers who become billionaire twenty-somethings. These narratives of success focus on lavish lifestyles and all too often leave out the failures and struggles that are part and parcel of any success.

If we want our classrooms to be engaging, success must be redefined to include failure, and failure must be redefined to be the normal, inevitable experience of the person who takes risks and tries. In our engaging classrooms, as in the real world, success and failure must become two sides of the same coin.

When Sara Blakely was a child, each night at the dinner table, her father would ask her and her brother what they failed at that day. If they answered "nothing," he would be disappointed. If they had a story of failure to share, he'd high-five them and beam with pride. In the Blakely household, failure said nothing of a person's ability to succeed, and said everything about a person's courage to try (Frank, 2013). The ultimate effect was that Blakely disassociated failure with outcomes and associated it strictly with a lack of trying. Talk about a Quad D attitude.

This clearly had its impact on Blakely, who would eventually create Spanx, the women's slimming shapewear brand that changed the hosiery landscape. But this was only after being rejected by every last hosiery mill in North Carolina (home to most of America's hosiery producers). After all the other doors were slammed in her face, Blakely was finally able to change the mind of one mill operator (Blakely, n.d.).

By the time Blakely was 42, she was the first female billionaire to sign Bill and Melinda Gates's and Warren Buffett's Giving Pledge. This, the result of her fearlessness in the face of so-called failure and resilience amid setbacks, put her at the helm of her own multibillion-dollar company (Wirthman, 2013).

I encourage you to try a similar approach in your classroom. Instead of saying failure is not an option, tell your students failure is always an option! Failure is always a possibility for those who try. And in the well-developed classroom, we want and encourage our students to try. Ask your students regularly to share their failures with the class so that it can lose its stigma and shame. Help students shed the notion that failure is something that defines a person or says something about his or her abilities. Instead, repeatedly remind them that success is possible only by way of the valuable insights, learning, and fortitude that failure provides.

When we destigmatize failure and make success something attainable, we help create a learning environment where students feel more comfortable and confident in taking risks. When they know failures will not define them, they know they can proceed with agency, aware that they will maintain their self-respect despite inevitable setbacks and speed bumps. They also understand that they will maintain a respect for their peers when they hit speed bumps, and their peers will extend the same respect to them. When students do not fear judgment when failing, the environment becomes safe and conducive to risk-taking, tinkering, and experimentation.

Within this kind of learning environment, failure is not an endpoint. It does not mean one has to give up. It's an indication that some shift in strategy or approach is needed. Then, success becomes the thing students feel when they've maintained their agency through setbacks and persevered through to achievement. As the facilitator of an engaging learning environment, we teachers must take care to put in place classroom procedures that are clear, and also clearly flexible in order to leave room for students to struggle productively, change course where needed, and eventually get themselves to task completion.

Learner Engagement Indicator: Formative Processes and Tools

Feedback is the breakfast of champions. —Ken Blanchard

When failure and success are normalized in our classroom, students will naturally feel less anxiety around formative assessments. This is the goal, as it is performance data and feedback that unlock the door to improvement and progress toward goals.

Thomas Edison famously said: "I have not failed 10,000 times. I have not failed once. I have succeeded in proving that those 10,000 ways will not work. When I have eliminated the ways that will not work, I will find the way that will work." He was referring to the fact that he made 10,000 prototypes for the lightbulb before finally arriving at the version that worked. What many would have interpreted as 9,999 failures, Edison saw as 9,999 useful bits of instant feedback. Each time Edison did not get the lightbulb quite right, he got more data that would help him get closer to the version that would stick. And he iterated—fast.

Data is inherently neutral; it's humans who put judgments on it. Data doesn't tell us we're not good at something; we project that onto data.

Assessments, even those that reveal a regression or a flatline, are nothing more than information that can help empower informed agency. When we don't routinely use formative processes and tools in our classroom, we deny our students helpful insights that they can use to make strategic improvements. Assessments promote self-awareness and self-reflection. And it is only through these facets of agency that learners can see where they are in progress toward goals.

If you've been subjected to annual performance reviews, you know the dread and anxiety that surrounds them. The feedback is often outdated and comes far after the recipient has any ability to change course. They can also feel like an attack or a string of criticisms, which may be attributed to the infrequency with which reviews take place. There's a school of thought that says performance reviews in the workplace should happen weekly, or even daily, to help normalize them. They are then stripped of their power to induce apprehension, and their negative charge is neutralized. By nature, what was once a person talking at another becomes a conversation; the recipient is now operating within a timeframe where she can act on the feedback and make improvements in real time.

If we are used to regular feedback, it begins to feel less personal and more like an exchange about the information data provides. Frequency is everything when it comes to effective formative assessments.

When we as teachers can regularly support our students through the self-reflection and self-awareness process, we can help them see both as a less scary exercise. Initially, many students might feel ashamed or uncomfortable discussing stalled progress. As I've said again and again, by inviting students into the whys of our rigorous and relevant tools, only then can we engage them in the process. Frame assessments as holders of information that are meant only to help students self-reflect. Contextualize self-reflection and self-awareness within its many lifelong benefits; make these concepts relevant to them by explaining how these facets of agency are what empower us to make the necessary changes to the pursuit of our goals and dreams. Remove the fear of assessments by being transparent with their ultimate purpose and intention.

It's our job as teachers to use assessments to differentiate and individualize learning. It's not enough just to talk through assessment data with a student; we then must devise a path forward with that student to tweak instructional pacing and design to help the student make improvements. We must also look for data that shows when a student is not being challenged, and then work with them to increase the rigor and relevance of the student's learning opportunities. Remember that assessments don't just show learning plateaus; they can also reveal boredom.

What's really important here is that any plan to move forward is made with the student's full utilization of his or her agency. Assessments provide a great opportunity for us teachers to acknowledge, respect, and incorporate students' agency into instructional differentiation. Make them feel part of the process. Ask them where they think they are struggling and excelling. Ask them what they think they need to improve or feel more challenged. Ask them what they see as not working for them and what they know to be more helpful to them. Give them choice and voice. Then apply your experience and expertise to craft with each student a plan that you both feel comfortable with and believe will support the student toward achieving learning goals.

The origin of the word *assessment* is the Latin word *assessus*, meaning "to sit beside." This perfectly captures the essence of how the application of assessment data should feel and look in the well-developed classroom: collaborative, supportive, nonthreatening, and empowering.

Knowing where we are is the only way to know how we're doing in our goal to become who we want to be.

Part Two

Strategies to Move Instruction
Beyond Quad A

Before we dig into strategies, let's refresh on exactly what a strategy is. A goal is that thing we hope to achieve. A strategy is *how* we're going to achieve it. Tactics are the *what*, the actions we'll take to support the strategy and achieve the goal.

The nine indicators of the Rigor, Relevance, and Engagement Rubrics are our nine strategies for how we will go about achieving our goal of a Quad D classroom filled with students and teachers with Quad D attitudes. Each strategy supports rigor, relevance, or engagement.

Remember that a Quad D attitude means you set realistic, achievable goals, and break them down into sub-goals as needed. You do not need to be a Quad D expert on Day One. Practice, experiment, adapt, and don't be afraid to fail. All we have to do to begin is move beyond Quad A.

I've structured the strategies to open with common Quad A thoughts and mental blocks. These thought patterns limit the teacher's capacity to intentionally design instruction that moves students toward Quad D. These thought patterns also limit opportunities for students to reach toward Quad D. Quad A thoughts keep the bar set at Quad A.

Each strategy includes a set of strategic moves to vet your instruction and check for indicators that it will sufficiently move students beyond

Quad A. Suggested tactics, tools, and techniques to support a strategy are woven throughout and denoted by **BOLD, CAPITALIZED TEXT**. Complete explanations of how to use these tactics, tools, and techniques can be found in Part Three.

Now, let's get strategic.

Chapter Five

Strategic Moves to Raise Rigor

Rigor Strategy 1: Thoughtful Work

Quad A Thinking

- My low-achieving students are not ready for rigorous work.
- My primary-age students cannot handle rigorous work.
- My students prefer work that allows them to just fill-in-the-blank.
- My students need skill-and-drill to fill in their knowledge gaps.
- I tell my students the content information they need to know.
- I wait until the end of a unit of study to give students more rigorous tasks.

Two Strategic Moves Toward Quad D

1. When designing student tasks—short or extended—be intentional about both the level of thinking and the level of difficulty. The level of difficulty and the level of thinking are not the same, but both are important when assigning student work. Scrutinize the learning tasks you design for your students by asking two critical questions:

- What level of thinking do I want for my students?
- What level of difficulty can they handle?

Level of Thinking. Recall that the Rigor/Relevance Framework uses the revised Bloom's Taxonomy to classify the cognitive processing that a student must do when completing a task. Your goal is to move student work beyond Quad A and toward Quad D, which means asking students to do more than recall and comprehend new content. Examine each learning task in your lesson plan for indicators that it requires thinking to move beyond recall. Revise it as needed to allow students to demonstrate their thinking by doing at least one of the following:

☑ *Analyze:* The task requires my students to take apart new instructional content and consider how the separate components connect to each other, as well as contribute to the content as a whole. You can promote this level of analytical thinking with tools such as the **$1.50 SUMMARY, CAPSULE SUMMARY, COMPARE AND CONTRAST CHART, CONCEPT DEFINITION ORGANIZER, CONTENT FRAMES,** and **SIFT, SORT, & SUMMARIZE**.

☑ *Evaluate:* The task requires my students to use a specified set of criteria (including criteria they generated) to determine the significance or quality of ideas and information that is connected to new instructional content. You can encourage evaluative thinking with **QUESTION FORMULATION TECHNIQUE, QUESTION ANSWER RELATIONSHIPS, PARAPHRASING,** and **N.E.W.S.**

☑ *Create:* The task requires my students to combine ideas and information in new instructional content in a way that allows them to stretch their creativity and/or originality. Ask students to represent their thinking by allowing them to synthesize ideas and information with **FOUND POETRY, DESIGN-A-WORD, PROBABLE PASSAGE, METAPHOR BRAINSTORMING,** and **QUESTION STEMS**.

Level of Difficulty. In *How to Design Questions and Tasks to Assess Student Thinking,* Susan Brookhart suggests that "to adjust the difficulty of a task, create tasks that differ in their requirements for prior knowledge, experiences, and interests. To stretch students to do work that is more difficult, design a task that is a step beyond where they are currently working, not a giant leap" (Brookhart, 2014).

In other words, to be intentional about the level of difficulty, teachers must know their students. What background knowledge do students bring to the new content? Where will they struggle, and how productive might that struggle be? How much support will they need from the teacher or their peers?

Do not allow the level of foreseen difficulty, however, to inhibit the opportunities for higher-level thinking for ALL students. No matter how hard it is, work that does not ask students to think beyond recall or application of knowledge is still low in academic rigor. It amounts to busy work, which equates to boring work, which often provokes behavior problems and withdrawn students.

Both the **GRADUAL RELEASE FRAMEWORK** and **UPSIDE-DOWN TEACHING** support teachers in adjusting the level of difficulty in a task. You can also create **ANCHOR CHARTS** for students to use as scaffolds when they are working independently. In addition, students working together as **PARTNER A/PARTNER B** or on skill-based or interest-based **NUMBERED HEADS** teams can support each other through tasks that awaken a more productive struggle with new content.

2. Deliberately open information gaps to inspire content curiosity and extend student choice. It might be counter-intuitive to recommend that teachers design spaces for information gaps in their lesson plans. Gaps are what we want to close and get rid of, right? If you have not read about epistemic curiosity in Chapter Two, do that before reading through this strategic move so you understand the power of using intentional, strategic information gaps. With the end in mind, you will be able to connect how epistemic curiosity can serve as both a precursor to and a byproduct of the learning tasks you design for your students, and thereby promote thoughtful work that moves toward Quad D.

Sometimes as experts in our content, we have little patience for gaps in knowledge. We give our students the answers. Then we give them tasks to check that they can recall the answers we gave them, and voila, that information gap should be closed. That is a perfect picture of Quad A thinking.

You want more. You want your students to want more. How can you do that?

- ☑ *Start in Quad D.* Give your students a task that requires a high level of rigor and application beyond your content walls. A manageable amount of productive struggle forces students to break down new content and ask questions (analysis); challenges students to assess what information gaps they have (evaluate); and grants students the opportunity to connect the dots in an effort to make sense of the new content (create). **UPSIDE-DOWN TEACHING** acknowledges information gaps so that students can discover what's important about new content.
- ☑ *Start with short, well-structured tasks at which everyone can succeed.* Success motivates learning. Some students have not yet embraced a mindset that *failure* is not synonymous with *finished*. Through the **GRADUAL RELEASE FRAMEWORK**, you can positively impact students' perception of themselves as capable and persistent learners, as well as increase their stamina to tackle more challenging content.
- ☑ *Invite student choice with the problem, the process, and/or the product.* Decide how much structure you want to define within the task you assign students. You can provide a little or a lot. You can tell students the problem, but let them have choice on the process to solve it. You can outline the process and the problem to solve, but let students have choice on the final product that will represent their thinking.
  - ○ *The Problem.* Guide students to identify the problem with **QUESTION FORMULATION TECHNIQUE** and **UPSIDE-DOWN TEACHING**.
  - ○ *The Process.* **ANCHOR CHARTS** remind students of previously taught strategies and tools. Through **GRADUAL RELEASE FRAMEWORK**, you "gradually" model the process by sharing your thinking aloud with students until

they are ready for you to "release" more responsibility to them.

○ *The Product*. Foster creative thinking and encourage students to pull from their own toolboxes when deciding how to frame and present their final products. Provide opportunities for students to explore a variety of digital learning tools. See ideas under Relevance Strategy 2: Authentic Resources in Chapter Six, page 94.

☑ *Teach students to generate the questions*. The **QUESTION FORMULATION TECHNIQUE** is designed to change the way students perceive and own questions. With a strong question focus, students articulate information gaps by prioritizing the questions that matter to them and revealing the misconceptions that cause confusion.

Rigor Strategy 2: High-Level Questioning

Quad A Thinking

- It is easier to check for understanding with basic recall and retell questions.
- I know what questions I want to ask; I don't need to preplan them.
- I use the questions from my teacher's guide to check for understanding.
- My students struggle to answer higher-level questions.
- My students do not know how to ask higher-level questions.
- If I let students ask the questions, they will not ask the important questions.
- I give my students practice test questions to prepare them for the state test.

Two Strategic Moves Toward Quad D

1. Preplan purposeful questions and the formats that you will use for students to respond. With so much content to "cover," it's easy to get stuck in the Initiate-Respond-Evaluate (I-R-E) spin cycle: the teacher asks a question, a student answers, and the teacher states if it's correct or incorrect and then goes to the next question (Cazden, 1988). To move your classroom out of this low rigor slump, you want to be intentional and flexible about when you will ask questions, what questions you will ask, and how you canvass for responses. Thinking ahead of time about each of these aspects of classroom questioning supports you as you support ALL students in moving to higher levels of thinking. In the absence of creating a question plan in advance of class, questions inevitably devolve into the I-R-E spin cycle.

- ☑ *Preplan when to ask the questions.* Use your teacher's guide as a guide, not a script, along with what you know about your students, their background knowledge, and your content standards. Consider the target goals and objectives for each learning episode as you annotate your textbook, your lecture notes, and even your PowerPoint presentation notes to indicate the stopping points when you will use questions to check for understanding. Record the questions you intend to ask in the margins, on sticky notes, or within the digital presentation. Keep in mind that student responses may reveal misconceptions, so be prepared to ask follow-up questions for clarification, elaboration, and justification.
- ☑ *Preplan what questions to ask.* Design questions to build on one another in a deliberate sequence. Preparing questions across thinking levels "can transform classroom questions into analytic tasks that require students to think at increasingly complex levels" (Marzano, 2013). Use **QUESTION STEMS** to help you with the wording of questions that require analysis, synthesis, and evaluation of information. Knowing the four categories of **QUESTION ANSWER RELATIONSHIPS** will be useful when designing text-dependent questions. "On my own" questions are great for activating background knowledge before new content is introduced. "Right there" and often "think and search" questions limit responses to the recall and retell level. When you want to move students to higher-levels of thinking

about the content presented, you want to ask an "Author and Me" question.

☑ *Preplan the response formats.* To move toward Quad D, you want to engage and stimulate deeper thinking from every last student in the classroom, not just those who raise their hands. Therefore, you must be intentional about the format for students to respond to your questions, as well as which format to use for which level of question. *After* you ask a recall or retell question, hold all students accountable for thinking about a possible response before you call on one student to respond. Do not waste instructional time having students break out in groups to discuss low-rigor questions. **PARTNER A/ PARTNER B** and **NUMBERED HEADS** work well with higher-level questions that require explanations and justification. **RESPONSE CARDS** (preprinted, student-generated, and digital response tools, such as Plickers) and **IDEA WAVES** are appropriate when you want every student in the class to contribute an idea or response to your question.

2. Teach students to analyze and create questions. Your students are not game show contestants poised to play "Guess What's on the Teacher's Mind" every time you ask a question. You want to move your instruction beyond Quad A, so you must move your students to think beyond the mindset of a test-taker in Quad A. You can do this by empowering your students to think like good test-makers. Show them the kind of analytical thinking that goes into generating effective questions so that questions are no longer something done *to* students, but *with* students.

☑ *Show students how to analyze* questions from their textbooks, their tests, their teachers, and their peers with **QUESTION ANSWER RELATIONSHIPS**. Even the questions you pose with digital question generators like Kahoot!® or Socrative® should be examined by students and classified based on the probable source of the answer. Of course, students can also analyze their own questions. For example, in one phase of the **QUESTION**

FORMULATION TECHNIQUE, students sort their questions based on whether the probable response would be *yes, no,* or a one-word answer, or if the response would require extended explanation or justification.

☑ *Show students how to create* questions around a central theme, focus, or learning task. They can use the questions to challenge the thinking of their peers with **QUESTION ANSWER RELATIONSHIPS**; to give purpose to their research and writing with **QUESTION FORMULATION TECHNIQUE**; and to make sense of notes they take in class and use for studying with the **FIVE R'S OF NOTE-TAKING**. At first, their questions may be recall and retell, but the **QUESTION STEMS** will support students in developing higher-level questions. With your support, students can create the test and review questions for **QUESTION CUBES** and digital question generators.

Rigor Strategy 3: Academic Discussion

Quad A Thinking

- When I let students talk, they get too noisy.
- Classroom discussion usually gets off track.
- Some of my students do not want to talk. They are socially shy.
- Everyday language is easier for my students to use when sharing ideas.

Two Strategic Moves Toward Quad D

1. Preplan groups and pre-teach conversation skills. In an effort to cultivate academic oral language within the classroom, more teachers are providing opportunities for students to talk. This might mean assigning a turn-and-talk response or assigning a collaborative group task, but "simply putting students into groups and giving them time to talk will not automatically result in higher-level thinking" (Gallagher, 2004).

If you want higher-level academic conversations that deepen content understanding, you must be purposeful about the types of groups you form and the protocols for conversation in those groups.

Groups. In *Where Have All the Bluebirds Gone?* Joanne Caldwell and Michael Ford describe five types of classroom groups that foster dialogue beyond the whole-class setting (Caldwell & Ford, 2002):

- ☑ *Paired groups* give half of the students in the class an opportunity to talk at one time, which can help avoid those overpowering or underrepresented voices in the classroom. These purposeful partnerships, such as **PARTNER A/PARTNER B** and **N.E.W.S.,** are not the typical turn-and-talk, as teachers consider both academic and social compatibility and deliberately assign students to work together.
- ☑ *Cooperative groups* work together with a common text to complete a common task. They are usually assessed as a group, but a teacher can hold all members accountable for thinking and working through the **NUMBERED HEADS** technique as students complete tasks like the **SUMMARIZATION PYRAMID**.
- ☑ *Collaborative groups* work toward a common task, but usually with individual roles or resources, as well as individual assessment. **NUMBERED HEADS** is a great technique for distributing those roles or resources. For example, each student might be assessed individually, although the group is working together on **QUESTION CUBES.**
- ☑ *Interest-based groups* incorporate student choice, and therefore the level of relevance and engagement tends to be higher. Again, **NUMBERED HEADS** can motivate accountability, as these groups can become more social than academic if not monitored.
- ☑ *Skill-based groups* are put together based on data that indicates the selected group members would benefit from special and direct instruction from the teacher. While skill-based groups must be both focused and flexible, they do not have to be less rigorous.

Conversation Skills. Now that your students are in purposeful groups, you want them to have purposeful dialogue. Academic conversations are an expected aspect of scholarly behavior. They require specificity in language, active listening, and critical thinking. They also require a certain degree of thoughtful control over non-oral communication. Academic conversations do not happen naturally for many students, so we must teach students how to embrace this scholarly behavior that is expected and respected in collegial and professional communities. In *Academic Conversations,* Jeff Zwiers and Marie Crawford outline five conversational "moves" to teach your students when and how to prompt and respond to peers to the end of logical and respectful academic discussion. To help students practice prompting and responding to each other, post sentence starters on students' desks or as **ANCHOR CHARTS** in the classroom. The five conversational moves for students from *Academic Conversations* are as follows (Zwiers & Crawford, 2011):

- ☑ *Elaborate and clarify* when more information is needed or the information shared needs to be more specific.
- ☑ *Support ideas with examples* by making connections to and from the focus text, other texts, the real world, or your personal life.
- ☑ **PARAPHRASE** to restate and clarify what you heard, what you read, or what you said.
- ☑ *Build on and/or challenge a partner's idea* to shift the lesson to a real conversation instead of shallow talk where you are just waiting your turn to speak.
- ☑ *Synthesize conversation points* for closure and summary of the conversation.

2. Make content-rich vocabulary and academic language accessible to all students. The depth of the academic conversations in our classrooms will still be limited if our students fail to use academic language when they talk with each other. I like to share Ludwig Wittgenstein's quote with teachers and students: "The limits of my language mean the limits of my world. All I know is what I have words for." I tell students that if their language is limited to "May I take your order, please," then so too are their opportunities in life. I tell teachers if their students' language is limited to what they use on the playground with their friends, then so too are the opportunities for rigorous classroom talk.

You can set the stage for more valuable academic conversations around content and learning tasks by giving students equitable access to content-rich vocabulary and academic language.

☑ Use the **WORD WALL WORKOUT** to help students "exercise" their vocabulary muscles with content and academic words you post on the wall. Make sure the words are bold and big enough for all students to see.

☑ Before assigning a task to students as individuals or groups, post **WORD BANKS** where students can work as a class to deposit academic words, as well as withdraw words to use in academic discussions.

☑ Use **RESPONSE FRAMES** as scaffolds for students who need support putting their thoughts into academic sentences. Remove the frames as students become more confident in expressing their thoughts on a high academic level.

☑ **CAPSULE SUMMARY, PROBABLE PASSAGE**, and **SIFT, SORT, AND SUMMARIZE** each require students to analyze content words, justify their thinking, and synthesize ideas either before or after a learning episode.

Chapter Six

Strategic Moves to Extend Relevance

Relevance Strategy 1: Meaningful Work

Quad A Thinking

- I have a lot of content to cover; we don't have time for creativity.
- My students need to build foundational skills before they try more creative tasks.
- I need to get my students ready to pass the state test.
- I assign more meaningful projects at the end of a unit.
- My students are not creative.
- My content has little connection to the real world. Students just have to know it.

Two Strategic Moves Toward Quad D

1. When planning your lesson, intentionally embed opportunities for students to practice skills that foster creative thinking. Dictionary. com defines *creativity* as "the ability to transcend traditional ideas, rules, patterns, relationships, or the like, and to create meaningful new ideas, forms, methods, interpretations, etc." Unfortunately, many students (and some teachers) associate creativity with "students who excel in the arts" or "come up with a one-of-a-kind idea" (Drapeau, 2014). With that mindset, teachers attempt to take the pressure off of students and ask them to demonstrate evidence of learning with a paint-by-number kit instead of a blank canvas for an original watercolor (Brookhart, 2014). Granted, that paint-by-number task may be high in rigor, but students will still find little relevance in the task beyond the grade assigned to them unless teachers leave some space for creative and original thinking.

Bellanca, Fogarty, and Pete define three essential skills students need in order to think creatively: the ability to generate, to associate, and to hypothesize (Bellanca, Fogarty, & Pete, 2012). But you do not need to wait until the end of a unit to let students practice these skills. There's room to emphasize and promote creative thinking skills in daily lessons as well as in culminating projects. Here are some ideas to get you started.

☑ *Generate.* Before starting a unit of study, use the **QUESTION FORMULATION TECHNIQUE** for students to work in collaborative groups to *produce* and *prioritize* questions that matter to them. Before writing responses to open-ended questions, invite all students to contribute to a class **WORD BANK** by *brainstorming* relevant content and academic words. Use **FOUR CORNERS** or **GIVE ONE/GET ONE** for students to move about the room and *list* ideas, examples, and characteristics related to content.

☑ *Associate.* Pause in the middle of a learning episode to allow students an opportunity to *link* what is new to what is known. **METAPHOR BRAINSTORMING** is a great tool for this. Engage students with the **CONCEPT DEFINITION ORGANIZER** as they *combine* examples and characteristics of a concept to *create* a definition that makes sense to them. Encourage students to *align* big ideas from a learning episode as they compose **FOUND POETRY** or **ROTATING ACROSTICS**.

☑ *Hypothesize.* After a note-taking (not note-copying) session, allot time for students to *synthesize* big ideas into a **$1.50 SUMMARY**. Before a learning session, give students key terms to sort and *speculate* or *predict* what they will learn in a **PROBABLE PASSAGE** or through the **SIFT, SORT, & SUMMARIZE** technique. Students can also share how they *interpret* the key ideas in a lesson by working in teams to design **TABLEAUX** or frozen pictures to highlight the big ideas.

2. Tell students a high relevance purpose for lessons and subsequent tasks. A learning task has a better chance of success when learners know WHAT they are learning (and not just a regurgitation of the standards) and WHY they are learning the target goal in the first place. The language in your standards helps you define the WHAT of a lesson and subsequent task; however, you must articulate the WHY when you plan the lesson so you can share it with your students when you present the lesson. If you struggle to discover the WHY yourself, work with colleagues and school leadership to explore the reasons your students need to learn the specific content. It's the WHY that determines how meaningful the lesson and task might be for students.

☑ *Not Meaningful.* You do not tell students a reason for the learning or the subsequent task, or you possibly do not understand the reason yourself, so you tell them:
   ○ We are learning/doing this because it's in the standards.
   ○ You are learning/doing this because it's going to be on the test.
   ○ You are learning/doing this because I need to give you a grade.
   ○ You are learning/doing this as a consequence of some undesired behavior.
☑ *Less Meaningful.* You connect the learning or task to your subject-specific content only and tell students:
   ○ You are learning/doing this because you need to know (subject-specific content).
   ○ You are learning/doing this because you need to show that you can (subject-specific task).
It's important to note that, while there may be moments when these tasks, whether low or high in rigor, are necessary to check for content knowledge, relevance remains low until students apply the subject-specific content beyond the subject itself.

☑ *More Meaningful.* You relate what students are learning to areas outside of your subject-specific content, and you (or your students) generate tasks that offer students the opportunity to apply the subject-specific content beyond the subject itself.

- ○ You are learning/doing this because it relates to (content) that you are learning or have learned in (another discipline). Let me explain how.
- ○ You are learning/doing this because it is what people in a (career related to the subject-specific content) do. Let me explain how.
- ○ You are learning/doing this because it will be helpful if you are called on to apply it (in a real-world situation). Let me explain how.

Relevance Strategy 2: Authentic Resources

Quad A Thinking

- There is no wiggle room in my pacing chart for bringing in other resources.
- If it's not in their textbooks, I give my students the notes they need to know in a handout, a PowerPoint presentation, or a video.
- I assign a research topic to my students.
- My students do not have access to computers outside of school.
- My students will not go to the public library.
- We don't go on field trips because my students don't know how to behave.

Two Strategic Moves Toward Quad D

1. Instead of *covering* the content, engage your students in *uncovering* the richness within the content through enduring understandings and essential questions. I remember writing my first Understanding by Design unit plan, mostly because I had the advantage of sitting in a brainstorming session with one of its co-authors, Grant Wiggins.

As prompted, I started with the end in mind and used my content standards to think about the results I desired from my students. My language arts class was exploring the concept of theme and preparing to read *Something Upstairs* by Avi. It's a captivating ghost story, but it requires some historical background knowledge to *uncover* its theme. I wanted to build a bridge from my subject content to the related social studies content to the novel's real-world significance for my students.

After discussing and brainstorming with colleagues about how best to build this relevance bridge, I settled on a quote that reflected the enduring understanding I wanted my students to consider beyond their brief time with me. I posted George Santayana's words in the classroom: "Those who cannot remember the past are condemned to relive it." Under the quote, I posed a few essential questions (EQ) that my class discussed and revisited both during and after the novel unit. One of the EQs—"Is learning to read a right, a privilege, or a responsibility?"— sparked so much debate that several students searched history books for related laws, brought in other texts that tackled similar themes, and even surveyed other adults and students in the building.

Of course, just posting enduring understandings and EQs will not make learning more relevant for your students. You must add resources to the equation. Students need resources to find evidence that justifies their responses to EQs. The more authentic the resources, the higher the probability that students will be "engaged in *uncovering* the depth and richness of a topic that might otherwise be obscured by simply *covering* it" (McTighe & Wiggins, 2013; italics are author's). Content-specific texts are generally designed to *cover* topics. A variety of primary and secondary resources are required to *uncover* those topics.

However, the presence of enduring understandings, EQs, and authentic resources can still keep learning trapped in Quad B. That Quad D digging and uncovering begins when students "read like detectives and write like *conscientious* investigative reporters" (Coleman, 2011) with tasks that require them to analyze and compare information found in multiple resources, evaluate resources for usefulness, and use multiple resources to create solutions to real-world scenarios. Consider these suggestions to get you started in establishing a culture of inquiry in your classroom.

☑ *Analyze.* Invite students to participate in shared research around the EQ. Construct **CONTENT FRAMES** on the classroom walls or through digital tools such as Google Docs and Collaborative Whiteboards. Students divvy up the research responsibilities, fill in the frames with research information, and reassemble to compare what they have *uncovered* to what their peers have contributed.

☑ *Evaluate.* With an EQ at the center, guide students to come up with a research question. Of course, the **QUESTION FORMULATION TECHNIQUE** is a perfect tool for this. Students brainstorm, categorize, and finally prioritize the questions that matter to them. Armed with their own questions, students assess a variety of resources that you make available to them or they find through their own digging. They annotate these resources to extract relevant information, deciding what to directly quote, what to summarize, and what to **PARAPHRASE**.

☑ *Create.* Instead of looking through resources to find evidence to support their opinions and arguments, students first survey the evidence in multiple resources. The students then synthesize the evidence with the original EQ and develop an argument or opinion *uncovered* through their research. Imagine starting with the evidence first and letting it lead students to compose an argument based on a deepening understanding of the content! That is Quad D at its best.

2. Use technology to engage students in learning tasks that require higher-order thinking. Somewhere along the journey to the twenty-first century, we got so excited about new technology that we forgot it is just a vehicle for learning, not the destination. Technology professor Richard Clark says it this way: "The media are mere vehicles that deliver instruction but do not influence student achievement any more than the truck that delivers our groceries causes changes in nutrition" (Clark, 2001). I recently watched students spend the majority of the instructional block answering multiple-choice questions via the Socrative® app. Students used their tablets to respond to the questions, but they did not use those devices to "do" anything with the questions. The presence of technology did not change them as thinkers.

In his article "5 Ways Digital Tools Are Transforming the Education Space," Eric Sheninger points out that "in an information-saturated world," our students need "tools that help them analyze and understand multiple representations from a range of disciplines and media, such as texts, data, and photographs" (Sheninger, 2016). Many students today are technology savvy, but instruction for them remains stuck in Quad A because they are not called to "do" anything with that technology that requires analysis, evaluation, or creation. Here are some ways I have heard and seen teachers use technology as a vehicle for higher-order thinking.

- ☑ *Analyze.* Students analyze the questions presented in Socrative® or Kahoot® using **QUESTION ANSWER RELATIONSHIP**. The multiple choices are not the possible answers to the questions; they are the four types of questions based on the relationship between the question and the resource for the answer (Right There, Think & Search, Author & Me, and On My Own).
- ☑ *Evaluate.* During a Mystery Skype, students in one geographic location strategically ask students in an unknown location twenty questions. Students work in specific roles to evaluate the answers and research possible locations of their Skype peers.
- ☑ *Create.* Students create the prompts and survey on Poll Everywhere and execute them to analyze and compare data. Students use Padlet to generate ideas that are shared on the class Smartboard.

Relevance Strategy 3: Learning Connections

Quad A Thinking

- My students do not have any background knowledge.
- My students have limited vocabulary.
- My students do not see any relevance to anything.

- I post my learning objectives on the board each day, and I read them to students.
- I am sure my students make connections, but I don't have time to check.
- I make my students write down their connections, but we don't have time to share.

Two Strategic Moves Toward Quad D

1. Make metaphorical thinking a habit in your classroom. Let me share two memorable moments from my experience as an instructional coach. The first happened while visiting a kindergarten classroom. The teacher was showing students the globe and how it represents our world. One student—who did not raise her hand—shouted, "I get it. The globe is like a soccer ball. The black part is the land, and the white part is the water!"

Ah . . . metaphors.

The second image is from my experience at an alternative high school. To help the teacher understand the techniques I was suggesting, I volunteered to model a lesson in front of her highly disengaged and frustrated learners. The **PROBABLE PASSAGE** technique brought out so much engagement that for closure, I asked students to compare the lesson to a food, a sport, or a color using the **RESPONSE FRAME:** "Today's lesson was like ___ because . . . ." One young lady quickly said, "Today's lesson was like tennis because we were going back and forth with how we agreed and disagreed." A young man said, "No, I think today's lesson was like lasagna. It had so many layers to it. We read. We wrote. We debated."

Ah . . . metaphors.

Metaphorical thinking is by far the best way I know to help students connect the new to the known. In *Metaphors and Analogies*, Rick Wormeli explains that "a metaphor basically reimagines or re-expresses something in one category (domain) in terms of another category (domain) to clarify or further thinking" (Wormeli, 2009). He explores various metaphorical devices such as analogy, anthropomorphism, hyperbole, idiom, personification, and simile. Each of these devices permits students to travel the imagination bridge as far as the students' own personal experiences will carry them. With metaphorical thinking, students can attach relevance to new content, as well as reveal confusion or misconceptions. I once asked a learner to compare what we had learned to a color. He told me it was brown and muddy because he needed a clearer understanding of what we were doing and learning.

Metaphors beautifully make the rigor and relevance connection. They require students to *analyze* new information, *evaluate* it for clarity, and *create* a new thought to express how well they understand or value the new information beyond the specific subject content itself. But metaphors take practice. Keep these two points in mind as you move to make metaphorical thinking a habit in your classroom.

☑ Give students the vehicle to carry the metaphor across the bridge. In other words, provide a **METAPHOR BRAINSTORMING** tool that tells them to what they should compare the new information, word, or experience. Students can also **DESIGN-A-WORD** with images and writing to represent the metaphors they create for content and academic vocabulary.

☑ Practice metaphors two or three times a week and let students share their own metaphors. With a **RESPONSE FRAME**, students can quickly write a metaphor on a sticky note and post it as they exit class. Encourage students to create metaphors to summarize new learning and to reflect on new learning experiences.

2. Share current events and invite in community members related to the unit of study. When students connect content learned to their own lives, they are "discerning patterns, seeing likenesses and differences, and finding the perfect slot for the new idea" in terms of the background knowledge they bring to the classroom (Bellanca, Fogarty, & Pete, 2012). However, in order for students to link new content to real-world applications, they must know something about the real world. Instead of complaining when students have limited background knowledge, teachers can deliberately and consistently build background knowledge for their students by reaching beyond the classroom walls.

☑ *Find a place and time in your classroom for current events.* I've noticed several schools sharing articles from www.newsela.com or playing clips from CNN Student News. While I applaud their efforts to expose students to what is happening in the real world, I worry when teachers turn articles into test prep questions and video clips into movie breaks. Move these tools beyond Quad A with high-level questioning or deep academic discussion.

☑ *Teach students to analyze photographs.* Use questioning tools to generate deeper thinking as students cut apart a photograph into quadrants and study it or draw conclusions about the images. Every Monday, as part of their online Learning Network, the *New York Times* posts a photograph and asks students, "What's Going on in This Picture?" (Learning Network, 2016). The site invites teachers of younger students and students age thirteen and older to post comments on the inferences and conclusions they draw after studying the photograph. The *Times* shares the caption and other information about the photograph the following Friday morning. I know a middle school that is doing this exercise in every classroom during the third block each Monday. They call it Mystery Monday. Each class shares their inferences on a designated bulletin board in the school. After the Friday explanation of the photograph is posted on the *Times* website, a literacy team in the school gives small tokens to the classes with the closest match.

☑ *Search for people in your community who hold jobs, make decisions, or solve problems connected to your specific content.* Invite them to be guest speakers for a "What Would You Do?" brainstorming session, in which they share real-world scenarios where they had to use their knowledge of fractions or argument writing or cell division, as examples, to solve a problem. The guests begin by presenting the problem to your students, who then use new content to suggest solutions before the guest "experts" share what they actually did.

Chapter Seven

Strategic Moves to Engage the Learner

Engagement Strategy 1: Active Participation

Quad A Thinking

- When I ask a question, I expect to see more hands go up to answer.
- It's usually the same students who volunteer to participate.
- Students struggle in my classroom when they don't pay attention.
- When I catch kids who are off task, I call on them to get their attention.
- I lead the lessons in my classroom.
- I am the expert in the classroom.

Two Strategic Moves Toward Quad D

1. Intentionally plan for ALL students to participate. It is not enough simply to *expect* that all students should participate or *hope* that all students will participate. Engagement is contingent on how deliberately you *plan* for all students to participate. While you do not want to force or embarrass students into participation, you want to discourage students from slipping into the role of tourists observing others as they travel through new learning. Optimum participation is planned through thoughtful consideration to a few questions.

> ☑ *Who needs the instruction?* If you are reteaching content based on low performance, identify the low performers and design small-group instruction catering to their needs, along with alternate engaging tasks for the rest of the students. Formative assessment results should dictate the design of your small, but flexible groups.
>
> ☑ *Will students work in groups?* Use data to pre-establish **PARTNER A/PARTNER B** and **NUMBERED HEADS** groups to ensure each student is progressing through new learning with one identified partner or group. Even if students will be assessed independently, allow them to work together to make sense of new learning. In other words, if you ask students to respond to a question, allow them to convene with their partner or group for support as needed.
>
> ☑ *How will I check for understanding?* Although it is more challenging to check for understanding in whole-group sessions, it can be accomplished with preplanned techniques. **RESPONSE CARDS, FOUR CORNERS, GIVE ONE/GET ONE,** and **IDEA WAVES** produce short responses from all students and provide a quick status check of the class. With **PARTNER A/PARTNER B**, half of the class can respond at one time. Calling on a few partners allows you to check for overall understanding before a more formal formative assessment. The same is true with **NUMBERED HEADS**, although fewer students are called upon to respond. Read "Check for understanding throughout a learning episode" on page 106 for more specific tools and techniques.

2. Minimize your presence as the class expert to maximize student contribution to making sense of content. At ICLE, we like to describe the four quadrants of the Rigor/Relevance Framework in terms of who is doing most of the work. As expected, the teacher is working the hardest in Quad A, where both the rigor and the relevance are low. However, simply raising the rigor or extending the relevance doesn't matter if only a few students are thinking and working. What matters is what the rest of the students are doing. Are they on-task and compliant? Be careful. They might also be complacent, unaware of a need or a pathway to improve. On the other hand, are they off-task and disruptive? Again, take caution. Is this a mask for frustration or even boredom?

In *Never Work Harder Than Your Students*, Robyn Jackson warns us that students are often "content to allow us to do the lions' share of the work" (Jackson, 2009). And why shouldn't they if teachers are willing to be the expert, the know-it-all, or the final word in the classroom? Not much thought is required to copy notes from the teacher's presentation. Not much patience is needed to wait for the smartest kid in class to answer the teacher's questions, or even for the teacher to answer the questions. If the teacher is monopolizing all of the discussion, summarizing all of the learning, and making all of the connections to the content, the students need only sit back and be entertained. (Unfortunately, some teachers mistake this for engagement.) Keep in mind that students take ownership of their learning not because their teachers are great entertainers, but because their teachers are great engagers of learning.

Here are some tools and techniques to maximize students' contributions in the classroom by inviting them to become savvier about the content.

- ☑ **$1.50 Summary**. Students compose a succinct summary that captures the most essential content shared in a lesson segment.
- ☑ **FIVE R'S OF NOTE-TAKING**. Students decide what to record as notes. They use those notes to make sense of new information.
- ☑ **METAPHOR BRAINSTORMING**. Students "design" academic and content words to display in the classroom. When these additions to your word wall are designed by students, the words "stick" with them and their peers longer.
- ☑ **QUESTION FORMULATION TECHNIQUE**. Students decide what questions will take center stage in reading and further research.

☑ **RESPONSE FRAMES.** Students share content knowledge in a structured sentence frame that is grammatically correct and emphasizes academic language.

☑ **ROTATING ACROSTICS.** Students work with small groups to identify the most important details in the content, identify one word to encompass those details, and create an acronym to represent those details.

☑ **TABLEAUX.** Students form statues that represent how they visualize the key components from a lesson.

Engagement Strategy 2: Learning Environment

Quad A Thinking

- I have a word wall.
- My classroom expectations are posted, but students don't follow them.
- A lot of these routines are too elementary for my older students.
- I expect students to refer to their notes when they get stuck or confused.
- My students don't respect themselves. How are they going to respect their peers?
- Most of my students won't even try.

Two Strategic Moves Toward Quad D

1. Use the walls of your classroom as scaffolds of learning. Walk in any classroom today, kindergarten through high school, and you will notice words posted on the wall, often labeled the "Word Wall." Sometimes it amounts to no more than visual compliance. (*My principal says we have to have a word wall, so I do.*) To bring that word wall to life, students must actively use the words during reading, writing, and academic conversations.

The same is true for the posters, charts, procedures, and routines teachers display and attempt to implement in classrooms. These tools come *alive* when students actively and consistently use them. These tools *thrive* in safe learning spaces where, although "the student's brain is concerned with avoiding the dangers of embarrassment, failure, or harm," the student is encouraged and comfortable to take risks (Jensen, 2005). Students know, and even expect, the teacher will allow them to struggle productively, yet intervene as needed when that struggle is unproductive.

Bring the walls of your classroom alive with **ANCHOR CHARTS**, **WORD BANKS**, **RESPONSE FRAMES,** and the **WORD WALL WORKOUT**.

2. Reframe failure as a positive catalyst for learning new content. Former teacher and MacArthur fellow Angela Duckworth describes grit as "passion and perseverance for long-term goals." She asserts that grit is not something we have to be born with, but rather something we can develop—something we can develop with and in our students (Duckworth, 2016). When students project mental tenacity in our classrooms, they set learning goals, and they cling to those goals through obstacles, through stumbling blocks, and even through what some may perceive as failure. The good news is that whether your students were raised in affluent or adverse environments, you can promote grit, resilience, and mental tenacity within your instructional design. In other words, you can intentionally plan for opportunities to engage your students in learning tasks and academic discussions that signal failure as inspiration instead of stagnation.

Here are a few ideas to begin establishing a culture of persistent and resilient learning in your classroom.

☑ *Begin with* **UPSIDE-DOWN TEACHING**, *which has risk-taking and productive struggle at its core.* Give students problems to solve before you teach them the skills to solve them.

☑ *Establish a safe environment for students to take risks.* Allow them to collaborate with peers when completing tasks as **NUMBERED HEADS** groups. Provide **RESPONSE FRAMES** to help students express their successes and struggles as they set new learning goals.

☑ *Share stories of real people whose failures have inspired them to keep trying.* For example, share stories about Madame Curie, George

Washington Carver, and Thomas Edison before asking your students to conduct science experiments—both predictable and unpredictable ones.

☑ *Let students generate a "Grit Pledge" for the classroom to inspire anyone who gets stuck.* Enlarge it and post it on the wall to read aloud as a class from time to time.

Engagement Strategy 3: Formative Processes and Tools

Quad A Thinking

- Parents and students only care about the grade.
- I check for understanding by asking if students have questions.
- I give a formative assessment at least once a week.
- I put students into groups based on results from state achievement tests.
- When students don't study, they cannot be successful in my class.

Two Strategic Moves Toward Quad D

1. Check for understanding throughout a learning episode. Summative assessments are like yardsticks. You use them to measure learning after the fact through a grade or a score on instruments such as a unit test, a culminating project, or a final exam. You evaluate learning with summative assessments.

Formative assessments are more like mirrors. They work alongside instruction to reflect students' understanding and misconceptions. More diagnostic and descriptive in nature, formative assessments represent evidence of learning during a lesson plan or learning unit. You validate the effect of your instructional design on its ability to elicit intended student learning with formative assessments. The information they reveal can then be used to make real-time improvements and enhancements as needed.

Checking for understanding occurs frequently in developed and well-developed classrooms, as teachers provide time for both closure and review. In *How the Brain Learns,* David Sousa explains how closure and review are different in terms of who is doing most of the work. The teacher is working during review, "repeating key concepts made during the lesson and rechecking student understanding." However, closure is the time for the students to work by "mentally rehearsing and summarizing those concepts and deciding whether they make sense and have meaning" (Sousa, 2011).

Several closure tools that allow students to reflect on whether or not they are meeting the expectations of your intentional instruction follow. Many can be implemented in less than ten minutes.

- ☑ **$1.50 SUMMARY**
- ☑ **CAPSULE SUMMARY**
- ☑ **FOUR CORNERS**
- ☑ **GIVE ONE/GET ONE**
- ☑ **IDEA WAVES**
- ☑ **METAPHOR BRAINSTORMING**
- ☑ **PARAPHRASING**
- ☑ **RESPONSE CARDS**
- ☑ **ROTATING ACROSTICS**
- ☑ **SIFT, SORT, AND SUMMARIZE**
- ☑ **SUMMARIZATION PYRAMID**
- ☑ **WORD WALL WORKOUT**

2. Use *effective* feedback to empower students and tweak instruction. In 2006, differentiation expert Carol Ann Tomlinson and backward planning guru Jay McTighe co-authored a text illustrating the power of combining "understanding by design" (UbD) with "differentiated instruction." In describing the impact of UbD on diverse learners, they suggested four essential components of an effective feedback system (Tomlinson & McTighe, 2006):

- ☑ *Timeliness.* The quicker the feedback, the quicker students can become aware of their performance and self-direct and self-reflect in terms of the target goal.

☑ *Specificity.* A score or grade does not adequately describe what the students have done well or what the students need to do to improve performance. Notice how the criteria descriptors in the sample **ANALYTIC RUBRICS** are specific enough to discern one performance level from another and thus self-direct students to improve performance accordingly.

☑ *Clarity.* Use student-friendly language when sharing oral or written feedback with students. Feedback is useless unless the receiver understands it clearly enough to know what to do to improve the next time. Invite students to help illuminate what proficiency looks like or sounds like by showing them examples or models of proficient and advanced responses.

☑ *Refinement.* What good is feedback if you cannot use it to modify your performance? Within your instructional design time, deliberately plan for students to act on feedback by adjusting their performance as needed.

Part Three

Tactics, Tools, and Techniques to Move Beyond Quad A

Warning! Read this section only *after* you've read the first two sections of the book. Avoid jumping straight to these tactics without first understanding how they serve larger strategies that serve a larger goal. Moving beyond Quad A requires that we ourselves become students of the Rigor/Relevance Framework, which means we are striving to model, embody, and mirror a Quad D attitude and approach to lifelong learning. Support your students and your personal goals by reading the book in full before digging into the tactics.

Don't begin at the end of the book; begin with the end in mind!

As you work through these 33 tactics, here are a few points to keep in mind.

1. Don't get hung up on what a tactic is called. You may call it something else, or you may have seen it somewhere else under a different name. Remember Shakespeare? "What's in a name? That which we call a rose by any other name would smell as sweet."
2. Modify the tactics as needed for your subject and grade level. Just be careful not to squeeze out the rigor, relevance, or learner engagement.

3. Look for one or more of the rigor, relevance, and engagement indicator strategies at the start of each tactic. This keeps the focus on how you can use each tactic to strategically move beyond Quad A per the rubric indicator.

4. In certain tactics, I will reference other tactics, denoted by **BOLD, CAPITALIZED TEXT.**

5. Pay attention to the italicized verbs in the descriptions of each tactic. These indicate student "moves"—work that requires their active participation and engagement—to intentionally model and monitor within your instructional design.

6. Be a teacher researcher. Look for the impact on student achievement. Ask your students for feedback after you try something. Don't be afraid to adapt tactics to fit your students' and your classroom's needs.

Chapter Eight

Tactics, Tools, and Techniques

Tactic 1: $1.50 Summary

- ☑ Thoughtful Work
- ☑ Meaningful Work
- ☑ Active Participation
- ☑ Formative Processes and Tools

Students *analyze* a learning segment and *compose* a single statement that captures the most essential concepts shared. Instead of asking students to write a summary sentence, you limit the amount of words students can use, forcing them to filter out trivial details and make decisions about what's most important.

How It Works

With each word costing $.10, students are given a range of how much they must spend and how much they can spend when composing their summary sentences. For example, you might ask students to spend at least $.90, but no more than $1.50. That means the students' summary sentences should be between nine and 15 words.

Suggest partners and small groups work together to answer these questions as they compose their summary statements.

- What are the key ideas, and what links them together?
- What academic vocabulary did we keep hearing over and over?
- How is this new information connected to content we have already learned?

Other suggestions for implementing this tactic:

- Remind students that their summary must be a sentence, not a title. It should contain a verb and appropriate punctuation.
- Remain flexible. Allow students to "borrow" a dime if they need an extra word.
- When a great deal of information is shared, increase the value of the sentence.
- Write your own summary statement first. You do not need to share it with your students, but you should be aware of the level of challenge the summary will present for your students.
- When working with primary students, serve as the scribe and facilitator as you work with them to create a summary sentence together, while allowing them to make decisions about adding, deleting, or changing words.

Here is a $1.50 summary of this tactic: *With a restricted word amount, students demonstrate understanding by condensing key ideas into one sentence.*

Tactic 2: Analytic Rubrics

☑ Thoughtful Work
☑ Formative Processes and Tools

Students *assess* and *refine* tasks based on descriptions of selected criteria within distinct performance levels. Analytic rubrics do not focus on the task as a whole, and are, therefore, more diagnostic for the teacher and the student.

Here are four essential steps to employ when creating effective analytic rubrics.

1. *Identify the task and learning goal.* Use the language of your standards for clarity.
2. *Establish criteria to assess.* Your standards help to focus the criteria on what's important versus what might be trivial and not contribute to a student successfully meeting the learning goal. For example, if the goal is to write an informative essay, each criterion should address that goal. Setting one criterion for spelling, another for punctuation, another for grammar, and yet another for capitalization emphasizes a focus on the conventions of writing. Go back to the standard. What do students need to be able to do with informational writing? Unpack the standard to set criteria that supports it.
3. *Determine the levels of mastery.* Four levels generally work better than three. You can use levels that mirror performance indicators on your state assessments, such as Advanced, Proficient, Developing, or Beginning. Or you can be creative with labeling the levels, but avoid using numbers, as that makes the assessment more evaluative than descriptive for your students.
4. *Write descriptors for each criterion.* This is both the most challenging and the most important step in creating an effective analytic rubric. Clearly describe what student work looks like for each criterion at each performance level. Avoid unyielding descriptors such as "Writes five sentences in each paragraph," or "Cites two examples." On the other end of the spectrum, resist

terms such as *somewhat, all the time,* or *mostly,* which are too subjective to help students identify where they stand. Remember the descriptions are there to help students compare their work with specific performance levels so that they can make decisions about how to improve performance to advance or maintain level of mastery.

Keep in mind that students should ALWAYS see this type of analytic rubric BEFORE they begin work on the task. The rubric serves as a guide for students to set learning targets and make adjustments as they work through specified tasks.

Here are some examples to help you as you generate your own rubrics for and eventually with your students.

Criterion	YES...AND	YES	YES...BUT	NO...BUT	NO
Summarize the key supporting details and ideas.	**YES,** I summarized the key supporting details and ideas, **AND** my summary is cohesive and organized.	**YES,** I summarized the key supporting details and ideas.	**YES,** I summarized the text, **BUT** I included some unnecessary details or left out some key information.	**NO,** I did not summarize the text, **BUT** I did list some key details.	**NO,** I did not summarize the text.

Constructive Response Rubric				
Task: Construct a written response that includes the question restated, a logical/correct answer, and supporting textual evidence.				
Criteria	Advanced	Proficient	Developing	Beginning
Flip the question into a statement.	☐ Writer incorporates restated question and logical answer in an insightful introduction.	☐ Writer flips question into a statement.	☐ Writer copies question verbatim.	☐ Writer omits any reference to question.
Answer question logically/ Correctly.		☐ Writer provides a logical/ correct answer.	☐ Writer gives a vague or limited answer.	☐ Writer gives an illogical or irrelevant answer.
Tell/cite two-three textual details as evidence to support a logical answer.	☐ Writer integrates paraphrased, summarized, and/or quoted strong and thorough textual evidence in a cohesive and organized manner.	☐ Writer paraphrases, summarizes, and/or quotes sufficient and relevant textual evidence to support a logical answer.	☐ Writer provides limited textual evidence. ☐ Writer rewrites text excerpt(s) without showing connections to a logical answer.	☐ Writer's evidence is missing, unrelated, or not supported by the text(s).

Tactic 3: Anchor Charts

☑ Thoughtful Work
☑ Academic Discussion
☑ Learning Environment
☑ Formative Processes and Tools

Students *monitor* and *evaluate* their own understanding of previously taught lessons. These teacher-created charts provide academic support, especially for visual learners and students working independently. Students "hold on" to anchor charts that act as scaffolds and reinforce new content, strategies, and examples. Anchor charts are beneficial even in secondary classrooms where students are taking notes. Students who have useful and organized notes can use those notes for unguided practice away from your classroom; the anchor chart ensures equitable access for all learners in the room.

To generate strong and meaningful anchor charts, follow these suggested steps.

1. Preplan information to record on anchor chart. This could be information copied from an instructional source, even a colleague's anchor chart. Produce the text or visual aids ahead of time to attach to the chart during the lesson.
2. Develop the chart in front of your students, as you strategically move through the lesson. (If you teach a subject in more than one class session a day, recreate the chart for each class.) This is the advantage of teacher-generated charts over store-bought charts. Students hear you "thinking aloud" as you assemble the chart in front of them. That "teacher think-aloud" supports audio learners and demystifies the thinking for all learners.
3. Place the chart so that it is accessible to all students. Keep it on display for a specific unit of study or for as long as needed to support students. Again, let the students see where you physically place the chart.
4. Refer to the chart in subsequent lessons, and encourage students to refer to it for support as needed.

THINK BIG!

WHAT: Find the big ideas in what you are reading.

WHY: Everything else in the text supports the main idea. You must be able to find the main idea in order to complete other reading tasks.

HOW: Try one of these strategies:

*Look for repeated words or ideas.

*Turn the title or heading into a question and answer it.

*Create a title for what you read.

*Determine the author's purpose.

*Choose words/images that stand out.

*Look for changes in font style, size, or color.

Tactic 4: Capsule Summary

☑ Thoughtful Work
☑ Academic Discussion
☑ Formative Processes and Tools

Students *condense* key ideas and supporting details in spoken and/or written summaries. To introduce this technique, remind students that a capsule is a container with only enough room to enclose the most essential parts. For example, a pill capsule holds a dose of medicine. A capsule, like a summary, is compact and brief, which is why capsule summary is a practical mechanism for teaching students how to write efficient summaries.

Keep instruction for capsule summary simple and strategic by following this basic sequence.

1. Students nominate words to place in the capsule summary. The words are associated with the essential question or topic. Use an **IDEA WAVE** to record suggested terms. Tell students how many words you will allow in the capsule. (Five to ten work best.) Facilitate classroom discussion and debate about which words to keep and which words to "vote out of" the capsule. As students make suggestions, they must defend their thinking, which means they must interact with the content. For example, a student working to summarize a lesson on ratios might suggest eliminating the term *divide* because the term *quotient* suggests that division is occurring. Another student might argue to keep *divide* because it is significant to understanding the relationship of the numbers in the ratio. As the facilitator, encourage students to challenge the thinking of their peers before the final vote on whether the word stays or goes.

2. Display the final capsule words for all students to see and use in a conversation with a partner. Each student should utilize all of the terms as they talk about key points from the original text or presentation. If needed, model this "talk" with students to emphasize how (a) it is not a recitation of definitions, but

rather a dialogue about the content using the terms, and (b) they should refer back to notes and texts when unsure about how the words are connected.

3. Without looking at the original text or presentation, students should now record a summary of the new content. Because they were more astute when selecting the words for the capsule, students will tend to avoid adding irrelevant details when writing their summaries. More important, because they were able to verbally explore the connections among the capsule words, students will tend to transfer those connections to paper.

Tactic 5: Compare and Contrast Chart

☑ Thoughtful Work
☑ Meaningful Work

Students *dissect* two concepts by evaluating similarities and differences based on specific criteria. The most significant distinction between this tool and other organizers that compare and contrast is that the Compare and Contrast Chart asks students to identify an explicit criterion for each difference highlighted.

How It Works

You can give students the criteria you want them to use as they examine the two concepts. However, if you want to promote more rigorous thinking, challenge students to identify the criteria they will use in determining how the two concepts are different.

I like to model how to use this tool by asking students to compare and contrast two familiar concepts. For example, you can ask students to engage in a purposeful conversation with a peer to determine how they are alike and different when it comes to specific criteria such as birthday, number of siblings, dreams, etc. When you don't dictate the parameters of the comparisons, you empower students to make more relevant connections.

Here is an example of a completed compare and contrast chart examining the frog and the toad.

Compare and Contrast Chart		
Concept 1 Frog		**Concept 2** Toad

How are they different?

when it comes to...

moist and smooth	skin texture	dry and bumpy
likes to stay in or near the water	habitat	likes to stay on land; prefers it dry
a flat body	body	a fat body
long and strong legs good for jumping	legs	short legs good for walking

How are they alike?

amphibians
eat insects and worms
lay eggs

Once the chart is completed, extend thinking by asking students to use the information gathered to write a poem from the perspectives and voices of the two points of comparison. Two students take turns reading one line at a time in the role of one of the concepts, but reading together when the lines are in the middle, representing similarities.

Frog and Toad Poem for Two Voices		
Frog	**Both**	**Toad**
	We are amphibians. We can live on land or in water.	
But I like the water. It keeps my skin moist and smooth.		Not me. I prefer the land. See my dry and bumpy skin.
Watch me. I have strong hind legs. They are good for jumping.		So my legs are short. They are still good for walking.
	Yum. We love insects and worms.	

Tactic 6: Concept Definition Organizer

☑ Thoughtful Work
☑ Meaningful Work

Students *generate* original definitions or descriptions for key concepts. Making sense of abstract ideas can be challenging for students as they are learning new content. Dictionary or glossary definitions are often too concise for students to make relevant connections. While you could compose a user-friendly definition of a concept to share with your students, the reward will be greater when your students develop their own definition with your guidance. A concept definition organizer, an example of which follows, is a useful tool to help students structure their thought processes as they grasp concepts in new or deeper ways.

How It Works

I recommend the following sequence, which corresponds to the accompanying organizer chart example from one of my class sessions, when supporting students to explore deeper meaning for essential concepts.

1. Begin with an activity that allows students to explore the concept. In the chart example, the focus concept was humor. I began this exercise by intentionally sharing with my students a few jokes, humorous pictures, and poetry written in a humorous tone. After showcasing your chosen focus concept—with words, images, poems, or whatever feels appropriate, taking care not to define it—explain to your students that their goal is to "define" that concept. To begin, ask them to write the focus concept in the chart box labeled "1. What is the Concept?"

2. Per step 1, your students should have several concrete examples of the focus concept. Ask them to select three that resonate and make sense to them. Students should then write down their selected examples in the three circles under heading #2 in the chart. Students can use illustrations, equations, symbols, or words to represent the concrete examples.

3. Guide students as they examine the three concrete examples and look for properties or characteristics shared by all three. Ask them to list these similarities in the boxes under heading #3.

4. Next, ask students to identify a category or group for the concept by completing the sentence, "This concept is an example of ___." Students then record their answer under heading #4.

5. Finally, support students as they create new definitions for the focus concept by combining the concept, characteristics, and category into a user-friendly descriptive definition. Students record their new and original definition under heading #5. They can elaborate on their new definitions by adding one or more of the concrete examples.

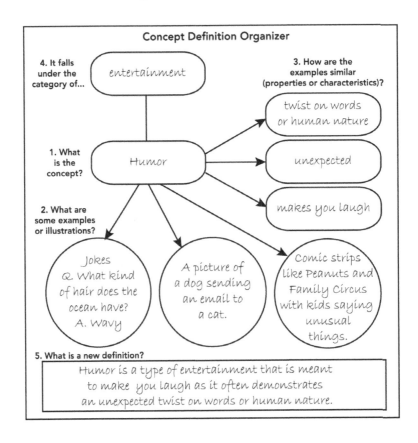

Concept Definition Organizer

4. It falls under the category of... — *entertainment*

3. How are the examples similar (properties or characteristics)?
- *twist on words or human nature*
- *unexpected*
- *makes you laugh*

1. What is the concept? — *Humor*

2. What are some examples or illustrations?
- *Jokes Q. What kind of hair does the ocean have? A. Wavy*
- *A picture of a dog sending an email to a cat.*
- *Comic strips like Peanuts and Family Circus with kids saying unusual things.*

5. What is a new definition?
Humor is a type of entertainment that is meant to make you laugh as it often demonstrates an unexpected twist on words or human nature.

Tactic 7: Content Frames

☑ Thoughtful Work
☑ Authentic Resources

Students *survey* two or more related items for similar and different features. The results are recorded in an organized frame that provides students with a comprehensive view of how the items are connected within the instructional content. While students may "build" individual content frames, large bulletin board size content frames encourage collaborative and shared research.

How It Works

To construct the frame, create a table and, in the first column, fill in the items to compare: e.g., characters, presidents, geometric shapes, plants, animals, rocks. Next, generate for your students (or with your students to encourage ownership) the features to use when researching each item. List those features across the top row. (Note: you can list the items across the top row and the features down the first column.) Now it's time for students to research the items and fill in the chart with "content" they uncover.

Suggestions for maximizing use of the content frames:

- Don't wait until the end of a unit to use the frame. Develop the frame with your students at the start of the unit, giving purpose to upcoming reading and research. Have students fill in the frames as they uncover and discover new content.
- Divvy up the work by assigning each group an item or a feature to research.
- Remind students to cite resources and page numbers when posting research content in case it needs to be verified or used for future writing. For younger students, I provide a mini-picture of the cover of the books we are using for research. When they post content, they affix the picture of the book cited to applicable content in the frame.

- Provide time for student researchers to explain the content they have posted.
- Teach **PARAPHRASING** skills to help students make sense of new information and to avoid plagiarism when filling in the content frames.
- Allow students to use the content frames on upcoming tests and writing tasks.
- Ask students to discuss and write possible generalizations formed when examining the completed frames.

In the following example, kindergarten students studying various insects worked as a class to complete this content frame. Each student then chose one insect to write about using the information in the frame.

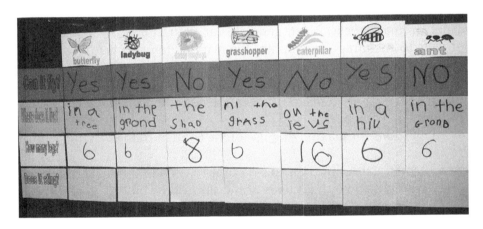

	butterfly	ladybug		grasshopper	caterpillar		ant
Can it fly?	Yes	Yes	No	Yes	No	Yes	NO
Where does it live?	in a tree	in the grond	the shad	ni the grass	on the leves	in a hiv	in the grond
How many legs?	6	6	8	6	16	6	6
Does it sting?							

As another example, students can fill in this frame with content learned during a unit on explorers.

Name of Explorer	Born/ Died	Land Explored	Main Challenges	Big Successes	Interesting Trivia
Ferdinand Magellan					
Christopher Columbus					
Matthew Henson					

Tactic 8: Design-a-Word

☑ Thoughtful Work
☑ Learning Connections

Students *incorporate* metaphors into visual displays of content words. The resulting product is sure to add spark to your classroom word wall. This tactic can be repeated several times throughout the school year. It's a great way to celebrate the vocabulary students already know and are learning about a topic.

How It Works

The visual displays generally take one to three 40-minute class periods to complete, depending on the degree of description you want for each target word. Be sure to include time for students to explain their word designs.

Students work as collaborative teams to complete these tasks:

1. Choose one content word. Give students options from words that (a) students know to some degree and can explain to others, or (b) students have questions about and require their deeper understanding.

2. Write about the word. Allow each team time to look through related books, chapters, or notes and jot down words and phrases connected with their target content term. Give each team a **METAPHOR BRAINSTORMING** chart, illustration, or frame to suggest images to "carry" the metaphors for their target term. Remind them that this is brainstorming; suggest that they write down all ideas, knowing that some of the metaphors may not work. Finally, tell each team to combine their notes and metaphors to create a single descriptive writing piece about their target word. Encourage students to experiment with genre and voice when they write their descriptions (not definitions) of words.

3. Design the word. Divide your classroom or space into three work areas and rotate the following tasks:

Cutting Letters	Finding Pictures	Revising, Editing, Publishing
Provide stencils or a die cutting machine for students to cut out the letters for their target word. Have different color (and texture) paper on hand for students to select colors that represent their metaphors. Suggest students arrange and glue their target word in a way that might help represent meaning.	Provide a variety of magazines, newspapers, or access to computer clip-art. Suggest students identify a picture that connects to their visual understanding of the word. Remind students that the picture does not have to be an exact match for the word, but might be used to help explain or describe the word to someone else.	After students have revised their descriptions based on teacher or peer feedback, they will need to edit for punctuation, capitalization, grammar, and spelling. The published piece can be printed from the computer or handwritten with colorful markers or pencils.

As an alternative to writing full descriptions of the target terms, students can simply design the letters for a word *or* design the letters, find a picture, and write a statement connecting the picture to the target word. Here is an example of a word "designed" for a math classroom.

Tactic 9: Five R's of Note-Taking

☑ High-Level Questioning
☑ Active Participation

Students *transform* notes into meaningful study tools. Note-taking sessions remain stuck in Quad A when students "copy" notes composed by the teacher. In order for the notes to be relevant to students, students themselves must decide the words, illustrations, icons, and symbols to record. If you have information that must be shared verbatim with students, then copy and distribute it to students. Avoid wasting instructional time with copying information. Instead, challenge students to make sense of content by extracting key points and supporting details, then synthesizing new information through questions and summaries.

How It Works

No matter which structure your students use to record notes (Cornell notes, two-column notes, graphic organizers, sketch notes, etc.), they will benefit from using the five R's as they process notes for future study.

- Students *record* key information in chunks, keeping in mind how the information is "structured." For example, if it is "compare and contrast," students should organize the notes to categorize the key ideas and details. If it is "cause and effect" or "sequential order," students might use arrows to connect and trace relationships.
- Students *reduce* what they have recorded to key questions answered or key terms to understand. In a two-column format, the reduction can take place in the smaller column. Students can also highlight terms or record questions in the margins. In essence, students are annotating their own notes to make sense of what they have discovered and uncovered during learning.
- Students *recite* what they have learned by going over their notes. For example, in a two-column format, students might cover

what they recorded in the larger column and attempt to explain the terms or answer the questions they recorded in the smaller column. Students can share their thinking aloud with a partner or think silently as they process their understanding.

- Students *review* the notes collectively by generating a written summary of the content learned. **CAPSULE SUMMARY** and the **$1.50 SUMMARY** are useful tools for students to capture the essence of the notes they record.
- Students *reflect* over learning by generating questions unanswered by notes, areas of possible confusion, connections to previous learning, and aha moments.

Tactic 10: Found Poetry

☑ Thoughtful Work
☑ Meaningful Work

Students *create* an original poem using words "found" in select resources related to content. Most students find this technique less threatening than creating a poem from scratch. After all, the words are already there. Students just need to rearrange them into logical poems that illuminate the target content.

How It Works

1. *Where do you find the words?* Students can work as partners, in small groups, or as a whole class to highlight 50–100 words from the target text(s). You or your students can also cut words from newspapers and magazines. Another option is to make several copies of 50–100 terms you want students to possibly use in their poems. You can cut the words up and place them into separate small bags for students to sort through.

2. *How do students incorporate the words into a poem?* The fewer the rules with Found Poetry, the more creative your students can be. I suggest students keep three points in mind when building their found poetry.

   a. Focus the poem around a central idea (related to content topic, if applicable).

   b. Try to add less than 20% new words to the poem.

   c. Explore creative techniques such as repetition, alliteration, and how the poem is presented on paper.

This is an example of a poem "found" with words from a first grade unit on the four seasons.

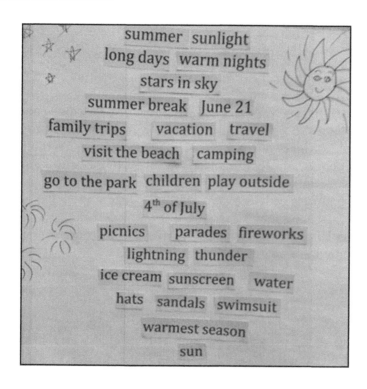

Tactic 11: Four Corners

☑ Meaningful Work
☑ Active Participation
☑ Formative Processes and Tools

Students *evaluate* their understanding or choice by moving to one of four possible corners in the classroom. This technique is great for formative assessment, but can also engage students in academic conversations around content. You present a question or statement to the class, and on your cue, students move to the corner that represents their thinking. Once in a corner, students can use texts to justify thinking, develop collaborative summary statements, or form interest-based groups. Four Corners promotes academic conversations, listening skills, and critical thinking for decision-making.

You can label your classroom with Four Corners in many ways. Here are some ideas to get started.

- Strongly Agree, Agree, Disagree, and Strongly Disagree to controversial topics
- A, B, C, and D associated with multiple choice responses
- The four question types in **QUESTION ANSWER RELATIONSHIPS** (Right There, Think & Search, Author & Me, On My Own)
- Four math problems (move to the corner of the one that challenged you the most/least)
- Four vocabulary terms (move to the corner of the one you understand the best/least)
- Four research questions to extend learning beyond content text
- Four seasons (move to the corner for the one you want to know more about)
- Four stories/texts/authors/artists/photographs/songs
- Four real-world connections or careers

Tactic 12: Give One/Get One

☑ Meaningful Work
☑ Active Participation
☑ Formative Processes and Tools

Students *brainstorm* a bank of ideas through academic exchange with peers. This technique engages students as they swap content vocabulary and concepts. Even if a student begins with only one idea, that idea can be shared for a second one, then a third one, and so forth.

How It Works

Begin with a specific topic about which students can brainstorm ideas. For example, you might ask students to think about vocabulary terms connected with the current unit of study. Once you've determined a topic, ask students to number their papers from one to twenty. You can begin the brainstorming session by suggesting an idea for students to record as a first idea. This supports struggling learners who may not be able to generate an initial idea. Tell students to record two to three additional ideas. Then stop them.

Explain the sequence for Give One/Get One.

- You will give students the signal to stand up and move about the room. For example, you might say a key word, ring a bell, or play a song. You will also want to tell students the signal to reconvene as a whole group.
- Each student should identify one other student and exchange one idea each. You may want to model how the exchange conversation might sound.
  - *Student 1: My idea is...*
  - *Student 2: Thanks. I didn't have that. Here's one of my ideas.*

- Students continue identifying one other student at a time with whom to exchange ideas. Remind students not to gather as a group, but to engage in a one-on-one dialogue with another student. Be prepared to walk around and facilitate to keep students on task and encourage full participation.

After five or so minutes, signal all students to return to the whole group. Use an **IDEA WAVE** to share results.

Tactic 13: Gradual Release Framework

☑ Thoughtful Work
☑ Formative Processes and Tools

Students *build* process knowledge with the teacher as a model and guide. This tactic is intended to support students as they move to the independent level when developing procedural knowledge. For example, when designing instruction to teach your students how to write a summary, your level of support decreases as students "gradually" become more proficient at summary writing.

How It Works
Nancy Frey and Doug Fisher describe five stages of the Gradual Release of Responsibility Framework as part of a formative assessment action plan (Frey & Fisher, 2011):

1. The teacher tells the students what they are learning, why they are learning it, and how they will be assessed. An effective way to establish this purpose of learning at the onset of a lesson is to share an **ANALYTIC RUBRIC**, which then becomes a tool to guide instruction and set learning goals.
2. The teacher models expectations through a think-aloud or a write-aloud in front of students. The students use the rubric to discuss the teacher's model.
3. The teacher guides the whole class as they work on the same process in a shared or interactive setting. This allows the teacher to give immediate feedback, again using the rubric as a guide. It is important to note here that the class works on the same process, but not the same topic you used in your modeled example. In other words, if you are teaching students how to write a summary, give them a different text excerpt to summarize. If you give them the text you just modeled, they will be inclined to simply copy it.

4. Small groups work together on the same procedural knowledge. Each group uses the rubric to assess their work. The teacher uses observations from these collaborative efforts to make decisions about further differentiation.

5. Students work independently on the same process. The teacher can provide direct feedback to individual students, while each student can use the rubric to assess his or her own work.

Sometimes teachers begin the Gradual Release Framework at a different stage. For example, the teacher might give small groups a task to complete to assess misconceptions or information gaps. See **UPSIDE-DOWN TEACHING** for a different spin on the Gradual Release Framework.

Tactic 14: Idea Waves

☑ High-Level Questioning
☑ Active Participation
☑ Formative Processes and Tools

Students *recommend* an idea to add to a class brainstorming session. This tactic encourages full participation. It works best when students share a list of words or phrases, instead of longer pieces of text.

How It Works

1. The teacher poses a question and gives students time to think and write their thoughts. Consider giving students a **RESPONSE FRAME** or prompt to record ideas for a more focused and structured sharing aloud.

2. A selected student starts the wave by sharing what she has written. The wave continues down rows or around tables. Expect some repetition, but encourage students to share anyway. If you have practiced response prompts with **PARTNER A/PARTNER B** pairs, tell students to use a prompt to elaborate or point out similarities if their ideas have already been shared. Allow five to ten seconds per student to keep the wave moving.

3. To end the wave, you might ask students to write a **CAPSULE SUMMARY** (if you recorded ideas on paper or the board) or a **$1.50 SUMMARY** of what they heard during the sharing session.

Topic 15: Metaphor Brainstorming

- ☑ Thoughtful Work
- ☑ Meaningful Work
- ☑ Learning Connections
- ☑ Active Participation
- ☑ Formative Processes and Tools

Students *analyze* the components and characteristics of content terms and concepts as they *create* and *defend* original metaphors. Instead of parroting definitions shared by you or the textbook, students clarify their understanding of new content by connecting it to familiar content such as the human body, cars, houses, colors, etc.

How It Works

To implement this tactic, supply students with a vehicle to help drive each comparison. The vehicle is the familiar image or entity in the comparison that "carries" the target term; by comparing unique characteristics or roles of the *vehicle* to similar characteristics or roles of the target term, the target term is conveyed in a new way that deepens understanding.

Consider this metaphor: "The Supreme Court is the backbone of our nation." The target term is *Supreme Court*, and *backbone* is the vehicle (or familiar image or entity) used to make the comparison between role of the Supreme Court and the role of the backbone. When defending this metaphor, a student might explain that like the backbone provides support and structure to the human body, the Supreme Court provides support and structure to the laws of our country. The resulting metaphor reveals interpretations, clarifications, and possible misconceptions about the target term.

You can offer students detailed charts or labeled illustrations that describe the unique characteristics or roles of possible vehicles they might use for comparisons. To increase student ownership, create these charts and illustrations with your students.

Vehicle: Parts of a House	Characteristics/Roles
Roof	highest point or top; covers, shelters, protects, conceals, limits
Front door and windows	entrance points, openings, passageways, beginnings, holes
Foundation	the core; supports, lays groundwork, acts as authority
Yard and fences	enclosures, outlines, limits, borders
Neighbors	proximity, connected, linked, dependent
Address	locator, direction, point, position

Vehicle: Colors	Characteristics/Roles
Red	energy, passion, anger
Yellow	optimism, cheerfulness, cowardice
Green	growth, nature, freshness
Blue	peace, boredom, depth
Purple	creativity, power, royalty

You can also give your students frames to begin brainstorming possibilities for target content vocabulary. Here is an example of possible metaphors for the content term *genre*.

Metaphor Brainstorming

If _genre_ were a color, it would be	If _genre_ were a food, it would be	If _genre_ were a sport, it would be
black because It goes with any topic	_eggs_ because you can make them in lots of different formats	_golf_ because It allows you to have your own form or technique
If _genre_ were a TV show, it would be	If _genre_ were a tool, it would be	If _genre_ were a month, it would be
the evening news because changes depending on the kind of day it's been	_hammer_ because depends on how you use it as to what tool it is for the moment	_March_ because it change depending on how the wind blows
If _genre_ were a toy, it would be	If _genre_ were a part of the body, it would be	If _genre_ were a number, it would be
Play Doh because you can shape it into many forms	_the eyes_ because they are a feature that tells a lot about you	_zero_ because it changes the value of a number depending where you place it

With the charts, illustrations, or frames to guide them, students are ready to examine, express, and explain their original metaphors.

Students *examine* select content terms in academic conversations with partners or small groups. Challenge students to describe, not define, terms by breaking each term down into smaller fragments as they share what they genuinely understand and what remains a bit fuzzy. Remind them to return to resources to confirm understandings and fill in missing information. The goal is for students to acquire a deeper meaning for the content.

Students *express* how the characteristics of each content term within the unit of study are similar to the characteristics of one entity within the metaphor frame. To emphasize how their thinking must go beyond a literal meaning for the content, I tell students to imagine how they would teach someone else what each term means by representing their thinking through an entirely different concept.

Students *explain* their metaphors to peers. Each explanation requires justification and textual evidence from the original content resources. I encourage peers to challenge each other's thinking by asking for clarification and elaboration of each metaphor. As students defend their thinking, they are formulating more authentic descriptions for each term. As students question the thinking of others, they are scrutinizing their own connections to the new content learned.

Tactic 16: N.E.W.S.

- ☑ Thoughtful Work
- ☑ Academic Discussion

Students *critique* the performance of their peers based on established learning goals. The feedback is focused, moving students beyond "I like/didn't like it" or "That was good/not good." This provides space for the students who receive the critique to respond, not in defense of what they have done, but in reflection of how they could improve their performance. Self-reflection gives the students an opportunity to set new learning goals.

How It Works
In the N.E.W.S. technique, students use four prompts to structure a critique.

N—I notice. This is a nonjudgmental statement that reiterates the learning goal and subsequent task and acknowledges the student's attempt to meet the goal by completing the task.

> *"I notice you cited textual evidence in your response to an open-ended question."*

> *"I notice you solved a multi-step word problem and wrote your answer in a number sentence."*

E—I enjoy. Next students tell their peers something they like about their work. This positive feedback should be authentic and focused on the learning goal, not superficial and focused on irrelevant features such as handwriting and neatness (unless handwriting and neatness are part of learning goal or task).

> *"I enjoyed that you included the paragraph where you found the textual evidence."*

"I like the way you circled key words in the problem before you tried to solve it."

W—I wonder. This is an opportunity for students to ask questions in order to clarify thinking or prompt additional ideas. Again, the wonder should relate to the learning goal and task. Suggest that students only share one "wonder" at a time, as critiques can become overwhelming when too many questions need to be addressed.

"I wonder why you didn't use quotation marks here when you copied verbatim from the text."

"I wonder why you used multiplication instead of addition to solve the problem."

S—I suggest/I still need. This portion of the critique follows the wonder statement with suggestions to tackle what might need to be solved or extended, as well as requests for clarification. At this point, students receiving critiques have the opportunity to respond by clarifying their original thinking and how *or if* they might use the suggestion from their peers.

"I suggest you use quotation marks anytime you directly quote a text."

"I still need to understand how you got the same answer as I did, but you used multiplication and you did it in fewer steps."

Tactic 17: Numbered Heads

☑ Thoughtful Work
☑ High-Level Questioning
☑ Academic Discussion
☑ Active Participation
☑ Learning Environment

Students *collaborate* with peers in small structured groups. Each participant has a specific role within the group. When consistently used as a classroom learning routine with a clear set of expectations, this technique promotes academic discussion and increases participation.

How It Works

1. Divide students into groups of three or four. Give each student a number from one to three or from one to four. To truly impact the academic discussion and participation, be intentional about how you group students. See page 86 for ideas on preplanning your groups.
2. Pose a problem or question to the entire class. Give each group time to think about and discuss possible solutions or responses. To encourage active listening and richer discussion within groups, provide **RESPONSE FRAMES** and **WORD BANKS**.
3. After groups have had an appropriate amount of time for discussion, identify one number to represent the group. The student with that number is accountable for sharing the response or solution generated in the group.

Other considerations when using this technique:

- Make sure you present a problem or question that is worthy of group discussion. Be wary of asking groups to spend collaboration time over tasks that mainly focus on basic recall and retell. To raise the rigor, present groups with opportunities to analyze, evaluate, or synthesize new instructional content.

- Post numbers on the desks in your classroom to avoid wasting instructional time identifying groups and members. To distinguish one group from another, color-code the numbers. In other words, designate a Yellow-1, Yellow-2, and Yellow-3 in one group. Label a different group with Green-1, Green-2, and Green-3 and so forth, with each group marked with the same numbering, but different colors.

- Use Numbered Heads to assign different roles to group members. For example, one student might be the "wordsmith," responsible for clarifying new vocabulary or unfamiliar words within texts. Another student might be the "scribe," responsible for recording the group's response on paper.

- Keep the groups' members and roles flexible and fluid based on the purpose of the task and your ongoing formative assessment of student performance.

Tactic 18: Paraphrasing

☑ Thoughtful Work
☑ Academic Discussion
☑ Authentic Resources
☑ Formative Processes and Tools

Students *clarify* meaning of texts they read in various resources or hear during classroom discussion. It's an effective technique for students to use when engaging in peer-to-peer academic conversations, when citing text-based evidence as justification for responses, or when making sense of assessment questions or directions.

Before teaching this technique to students, consider using a **COMPARE AND CONTRAST CHART** to explain the similarities and differences between paraphrasing and summarizing.

Compare and Contrast Chart		
<u>**Concept 1**</u> **Paraphrasing**		<u>**Concept 2**</u> **Summarizing**

How are they different?

when it comes to...

to clarify	purpose	to condense
phrase or sentences	original text	paragraphs or longer texts
about the same or more words than original text	length of resulting text	fewer words than original text
like a mirror to reflect exactly what the author said	metaphor to explain	like a filter to sift out everything but the most essential ideas

How are they alike?

Restate the author's ideas
Use your own words but not your own ideas

Use the **GRADUAL RELEASE FRAMEWORK** to teach your students a step-by-step procedure for paraphrasing until it becomes second nature and they no longer need to chart out words to substitute.

---

1. Write down the original phrase or sentence that you need to clarify.

    Tall hedges hid the house from the road.

---

2. Select a few words to substitute with synonyms. These might be common words or academic language. Use a thesaurus as needed to identify possible synonyms. Write those synonyms on a separate sheet.

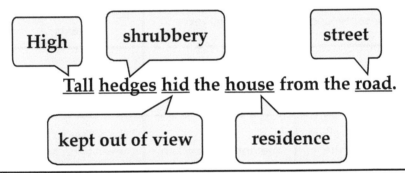

---

3. Cover the original text. Use the synonyms to "talk" about what the original sentence or phrase means. Check back to the original text to verify your understanding.

---

4. Use the synonyms to rewrite the ideas in the original text. Instead of just substituting the author's words when you rewrite, change the sentence structure to avoid plagiarism.

    The residence was kept out of view because of high shrubbery.

When working with primary-age students, modify the steps as follows:

1. Record the original phrase or sentence that needs clarity.
2. Guide the students to select four or five words to substitute out for synonyms. Underline those words.
3. Assign each small group or section of the class one of the words to explore (in a dictionary, thesaurus, or glossary) and find synonyms.
4. Record the synonyms on sticky notes and place the sticky notes over the words.
5. Guide students as they reread the phrase or sentence, substituting their synonyms for the original words.
6. Instead of asking these students to change the sentence structure, cover the text and post the synonyms for students to use in a **CAPSULE SUMMARY.**

Tactic 19: Partner A/Partner B

☑ Thoughtful Work
☑ High-Level Questioning
☑ Academic Discussion
☑ Active Participation

Students *clarify, justify,* and *expand* thinking during intentional peer-to-peer dialogue. Teachers who employ this tactic strategically pair students based on performance data and observations of social interactions. They also preteach students how to speak and listen to partners, particularly during tasks that require students to struggle productively with new content.

Forming Successful Pairs

- Make sure that skill level differences are not extreme.
- Conduct student interest surveys to identify common interests.
- Acknowledge student input when choosing partners.
- Assign pairs who enjoy each other's company.
- Cultivate a safe learning environment that teaches students to respect each other.
- Keep pairs flexible based on purpose of task.

Classroom Implementation

1. Designate which student is Partner A and which student is Partner B.
2. Pose question or problem.
3. Allow individual thinking time. This may include a written response.
4. Tell students which partner will speak first. Use **RESPONSE FRAMES, ANCHOR CHARTS,** and **WORD BANKS** as scaffolds to boost the academic dialogue.

5. Identify a few partner pairs to share their conversation aloud with the whole class. To promote active listening, have one partner **PARAPHRASE** what the other partner said. Include opportunities for both partners to summarize highlights of conversation.

Prompting and Responding to Partners		
Action	**Speaker**	**Listener**
Clarify thinking	Let me explain what I mean by... I believe/think this because...	In other words, you are saying... Can you talk more about...
Justify thinking	In the text, it says... An example of this is...	What is your evidence for... How does that example support...
Expand thinking	Do you agree that... What do you think about...	I agree, but (and), I would add... On the other hand,...

Tactic 20: Probable Passage

☑ Thoughtful Work
☑ Meaningful Work
☑ Learning Connections

Students *predict* probable content and focus before reading a selected text by:

1. critically *examining* key terms provided by the teacher;
2. *integrating* those terms into an original passage; and
3. *verifying* and *revising* the connections and predictions represented in their passages as they read through the original text.

How It Works

1. Choose 7–12 key terms that you want students to use when talking or writing about the text. Be very intentional about the terms you select. Consider terms that have obvious connections, as well as terms that spark debate due to possible hidden or dual meanings. Post the terms for all students to see or give each student a copy of the terms.

2. Place students in **PARTNER A/PARTNER B** pairs or small **NUMBERED HEADS** groups to examine and categorize the terms based on headings you provide. For example, before reading an informational text, you might ask students to sort the terms into six categories based on the type of information the term promotes (*Who, What, When, Where, Why, How*). However, before reading a plot-driven text, you might want students to sort words into four groups based on elements of a story (character, setting, problem, resolution). At the same time, a probable passage in mathematics might ask students to look for relationships among the terms without sorting them into distinct groups. During the critical examination of the terms, students should explain and justify the connections they make. Because

this is a before-reading technique, you will want to give students the option of having a category of Unknown Words, making you aware of terms that need further or deeper explanation.

3. Allow students to collaborate as they compose original passages using all of the terms provided.

4. Provide the original text or presentation of new content. As students are reading and learning, they can compare their probable passages to the original text or presentation, validating and clarifying information. To check for understanding of the new content, ask students to use the same key terms as they revise their passages in a **CAPSULE SUMMARY**.

Tactic 21: Question Answer Relationships

☑ Thoughtful Work
☑ High-Level Questioning
☑ Authentic Resources

Students *categorize* questions based on the relationship between the question and the possible source of the answer. This tool initiates a closer scrutiny of questions, as students consider what each question requires from the reader and what a question requires from the text. With consistent practice, students become more cognizant of the question-building process and *generate* their own questions to challenge peers and develop stronger comprehension of content texts and secondary resources.

Question Answer Relationships (QAR)			
In the Text Questions Are Text-Explicit (clearly expressed or fully stated)		**In My Head** Questions Are Text-Implicit (implied or not directly stated)	
RIGHT THERE Answer found in one place in the text	THINK & SEARCH Answer based on information found across a text or set of texts	AUTHOR & ME Answer based on reader's prior knowledge and textual information	ON MY OWN Answer based solely on reader's prior knowledge and experience

When introducing QAR to students, use the **GRADUAL RELEASE FRAMEWORK** to roll out the types of questions over several lessons. Here's a suggested sequence to guide students toward independent application of QAR to assess and generate questions.

1. Distribute a short text and 5–10 questions related to the text. Point out the difference between finding an answer explicitly stated in a text and having to use prior knowledge or experience to answer the question. Instead of asking students to answer the

questions, ask them to work with a **PARTNER A/PARTNER B** or in **NUMBERED HEADS** groups to discuss what each question requires of the reader. Does the question require the reader to use the text only (In the Text) or to use background knowledge to present an answer (In My Head)?

2. Distribute a short text and 5–10 text-explicit questions related to the text. Explain that while all of the answers can be found explicitly in the text, some of the answers are in one place. In fact, sometimes the words in the question and words required to answer the question are RIGHT THERE in the same sentence. Distinguish this type of explicit question from one that requires the reader to THINK & SEARCH across the paragraphs, chapters, or even other texts and put together different parts of the text to find the answer. Again, instead of asking students to answer the questions, have them collaborate to analyze, sort, and justify their sorts of questions as RIGHT THERE or THINK & SEARCH.

3. Distribute a short text and 5–10 text-implicit questions related to the text. Guide students in a comparison of questions that are not text-dependent and rely only on prior knowledge to answer (ON MY OWN) versus questions that require the reader to combine information in the text with prior knowledge to answer (AUTHOR & ME). Once more have students work together to sort the text-implicit questions into two categories.

4. Distribute a short text and a variety of questions, both text-explicit and text-implicit. As students work together to sort the questions into four categories, remind them to justify their thinking. Be prepared for students to disagree with you or their peers as they categorize the questions. Keep in mind that labeling questions is not the goal of QAR. The creators of QAR remind us the "emphasis should always be placed on the students' ability to justify their choice of QAR" (Raphael, Highfield, & Au, 2006).

5. Once students are comfortable with distinguishing one type of question from another, provide opportunities for students to work together and generate questions, challenging their peers

to both identify the QAR type of question and present a logical response.

6. Use QAR to support students as they review questions for upcoming exams. Present questions to students without showing the possible multiple choices. Have students scrutinize each question for what it requires from the reader before revealing possible multiple-choice answers. This technique is especially helpful when students are answering questions that are presented with accompanying graphics such as charts and graphs. Here are some questions to help guide thinking as students consider what the question requires the reader to do with the graphic.

   a. Can you point right to the answer in the graphic (RIGHT THERE)?

   b. Or will you need other elements of the graphic, such as a legend or title, to answer (THINK & SEARCH)?

   c. You don't see the answer in the graphic; do you need the graphic and your prior knowledge to answer the question (AUTHOR & ME)?

   d. Is the graph needed to answer the question (ON MY OWN)?

Tactic 22: Question Cubes

☑ High-Level Questioning
☑ Academic Discussion
☑ Active Participation

Students *defend* and *compare* responses to six rigorous questions based on a shared text or experience. This tool stimulates academic discussion, encourages full participation, and promotes a deeper understanding of new content.

How It Works

1. Use the high-level **QUESTION STEMS** to generate six questions that require students to validate understanding of new content through analysis, synthesis, or evaluation. Each question should require students to elaborate on new content and to provide textual support or evidence for elaborations.

2. Assign students to small groups. Give each group a copy of the questions and a die or paper cube with questions printed on it. Explain the expectations for the discussion:
   - *Take turns rolling a die. The number rolled by the first student is the number of the first question the group discusses. For instance, if the first student rolls a 4, the group will discuss question #4. That student becomes the first discussion leader and recorder, creating a bulleted list of notes as each member responds to the question.*
   - *The next student rolls the die and assumes the role of discussion leader and recorder.*
   - *Continue this process until all six questions are discussed and recorded.*
   - *All students must respond to each question, and all students must act as discussion leader and recorder at least once.*

3. The class reconvenes as whole group to discuss the six questions. Every student is responsible for representing their group's response to any of the six questions.

Once students are familiar with the procedure for Question Cubes, allow small groups to collaborate and generate six questions based on a shared text or experience. Give groups the high-level **QUESTION STEMS** so that their student-generated questions challenge the thinking of other students and require explanation and justification using text-based evidence. Groups exchange Question Cubes.

Here is an example of a Question Cube shared after students read the poems "Sick" and "Smart" by Shel Silverstein.

1. What is the theme of "Sick"?	2. How might the poem be different if the father gave his son a five-dollar bill?
3. What could have caused the boy in "Smart" to make the mistakes he did?	4. Prioritize Peggy Ann's health issues from least to m`ost probable.
5. How does the boy in "Smart" compare/contrast to the girl in "Sick"?	6. What intervention would you recommend for the boy in "Smart"?

Tactic 23: Question Formulation Technique

☑ Thoughtful Work
☑ High-Level Questioning
☑ Meaningful Work
☑ Authentic Resources
☑ Active Participation

Students *generate, analyze,* and *prioritize* original questions based on a question focus supplied by the teacher. After thinking through questions that are relevant to them, students can engage with multiple sources of information and take ownership of learning new content connected to their questions.

The creators of the Question Formulation Technique (QFT) argue that "the skill of being able to generate a wide range of questions and strategize how to use them effectively is rarely, if ever, deliberately taught" (Rothstein & Santana, 2011). When you include QFT in your instructional design, the students are doing the thinking and the working, naturally elevating rigor, relevance, and learner engagement in your classroom.

The Teacher's Role

Decide on a question focus (QFocus) to trigger student thinking. The QFocus is not a question itself, but a topic, image, or situation that your students will use as the focus for the questions they generate. The tighter the QFocus, the better the questions students create. For example, giving students "George Washington Carver" as a QFocus is too broad, possibly causing students to generate questions too extraneous to the biography unit of study that the teacher intentionally designed. However, "The life of George Washington Carver in his own words" narrows down the questions students might generate to ones that might be answered in authentic text penned by Carver himself. Before announcing the QFocus, explain the process students will use to produce questions.

The Students' Role

- Generate questions. Students work in small groups to brainstorm as many questions as they can. Consider providing sticky notes or chart paper to record questions. While you can list words that start questions (*who, what, when, where, why, how, do, can,* etc.), it is important that you do not interject your own ideas or examples for questions. Encourage students to take risks and persevere in order to "own" the questions they generate. Tell students a time limit (five minutes is plenty), and remind them of your expectations as they collaborate.
  - *Generate as many questions as possible.*
  - *Do not stop to judge, discuss, or answer questions.*
- Analyze questions. Explain the difference between questions that require *yes, no,* or one word responses (closed questions) and questions that require more elaborate responses (open questions). Discuss the advantages and disadvantages of closed questions. Do the same with open questions. Emphasize how both have value in authentic research. Tell students to work together to mark questions in one of the two categories. If needed, help students visualize the difference between open and closed questions by categorizing questions as "skinny" or "fat" to consider the amount of information each question requires. After students sort questions, show them how to change a closed question to an open one and an open question to a closed one. Suggest they change one or two of their questions to the other category.
  - *How old are you?* (closed/skinny)
  - *How would your life be different if you were born 100 years ago?* (open/fat)
- Prioritize questions. Direct students to put their questions in order of importance. In other words, for which questions do they really want an answer? Ask students to identify and share one or two of their top closed and top open questions. These are the questions that will provide the focus for the featured text or presentation. Of course, one resource will not answer all of the

questions students generate. What a wonderful opportunity to engage students with other sources of information!

This technique works well with all age levels because students are naturally curious, right? However, when implementing QFT with primary students, you may want to serve as the scribe as students generate questions, but allow the students to categorize and prioritize the questions themselves.

Tactic 24: Question Stems

☑ Thoughtful Work
☑ High-Level Questioning

Students *formulate* rigorous questions using stems that encourage higher-level questioning. This tool supports instructional design intended for students to engage in developing rigorous questions to challenge the thinking of their peers and take ownership of learning new content. Engage and empower students by asking them to sort the stems into groups based on the type of information sought in the question. Teachers can also use **QUESTION STEMS** when pre-planning a sequence of questions.

High-Level Question Stems

What are the pros and cons of ___?

How does ___ compare/contrast with ___?

What relationship exists between ___ and ___?

How would you categorize/classify ___?

Explain why it is not possible for ___.

What inference can you make from ___?

What is the theme of ___?

What is the motive behind __?

What are the components of ___?

What could have caused ___?

What is the most important ___?

What criteria would you use to assess ___?

Prioritize ___ according to ___.

What is the significance of ___?

What information would you use to support the view ___?

How would you prove/disprove ___?

How would you rate ___?

What would you recommend for ___?

How would you justify ___?

Would it be better if ___?

What would happen if ___?

How many ways can you ___?

Provide younger students with a Question Stem Chart such as the following. This will help them begin to build questions by combining a question word from the first column with a verb from the top row.

Question Stem Chart				
	is/are/was/ were	*do/does/did*	*can/could*	*will/would*
What				
When				
Where				
Who				
Why				
How				

Tactic 25: Response Cards

- ☑ High-Level Questioning
- ☑ Active Participation
- ☑ Learning Environment
- ☑ Formative Processes and Tools

Students *self-assess* and *monitor* content understanding as they compare their short answer responses to the responses of peers. As an alternative to traditional hand-raising, this tool is intended to maximize student engagement and to provide the teacher with a quick visual check for understanding or misconceptions. However, when the questions posed go beyond the recall and retell levels and students are required to explain their thinking to partners or small groups, response cards proactively engage students and give them immediate feedback to adjust their learning and participation as needed.

Blank Response Cards

The teacher distributes items such as dry-erase boards and pens for students to write on and hold up their responses as cued. For example, the teacher might present a word problem and ask students to generate an equation to represent the problem to be solved. Blank response cards allow for more efficient **IDEA WAVES** in class brainstorming sessions.

Preprinted Response Cards

The teacher anticipates a finite or defined group of responses and gives each student a set of response cards with possible answer choices printed on them (e.g., yes/no, true/false, living/nonliving, fact/opinion, x-axis/y-axis, judicial/legislative/executive, A/B/C/D, etc.) The teacher then presents various scenarios or examples, and asks students to hold up a card that represents their thinking. Many teachers preprint these cards in different colors. For example, *Yes* is the green card and *No* is the red card. This allows the teacher as well as the students to quickly scan the room and assess understanding.

Digital Response Tools

Each student has a clicker or device that transmits a real-time response to indicate student understandings and/or misconceptions.

- Clickers are given to each student and usually wirelessly connected to software on the teacher's computer. They collect responses and produce graphics that indicate how many students selected the possible answer choices.
- Clicker-free response systems invite students to respond via cell phone or computer. For example, with Poll Everywhere, students can respond to teacher-generated polls, multiple-choice questions, or open-ended questions. Both the teacher and students can see immediate results in graphs or in word clouds that represent top words used in open-ended responses.
- Plickers are unique coded cards assigned to each student. The teacher can then use the Plickers app to scan the cards for instant checks for understanding, resulting in real-time formative assessment data on his or her smartphone or iPad. The small print of the answer provides students privacy so they can answer honestly.

No matter which format you use, response cards summon higher-level thinking when the questions or problems posed ask students to:

- analyze and categorize examples
- associate specific characteristics with concepts
- evaluate explanations for accuracy or merit
- predict outcomes
- connect content to real-world scenarios
- share perspectives (not one correct answer)
- justify thinking
- generate questions to challenge peers
- self-reflect and self-assess performance
- suggest ideas to extend thinking

Tactic 26: Response Frames

☑ Academic Discussion
☑ Active Participation
☑ Learning Environment

Students *articulate* content understanding via framed sentences that emphasize grammar and academic language. Providing more structure than a basic sentence stem, these tools act as scaffolds to support and maximize students' contributions to classroom discussion and writing. Many teachers post generic response frames on classroom walls or bulletin boards to establish scholarly response as a classroom expectation.

After posing a question, provide a frame for students to fill in with vocabulary or ideas that best represent their thinking.

Vocabulary Frames

When you want students to demonstrate they understand a new word, instead of asking them to use the word in a sentence, give them a frame that places that word in a rich-context sentence. Assess their understanding by how they complete the sentence.

- New word: *essential*
- Context rich sentence: *One essential thing I do each morning is...*

When you want students to choose words from a **WORD BANK** or **WORD WALL**, give them a frame that forces them to select appropriate words and justify their thinking.

- The biome I think is most fascinating is the ____ because ___.

Generic Frames

Consider the type of dialogue you desire to hear in your classroom as you create a set of general ways for students to respond. For example, if the group spokesperson in **NUMBERED HEADS** is sharing the group's thinking, the student might use one of the following to frame the response.

- All of us agreed that...
- Some of us think...but others think...

To support students when working with partners or groups, give them frames similar to the ones shared in **PARTNER A/PARTNER B**.

Remember that response frames are support tools. Students need them only until they become confident in expressing their ideas at a more scholarly level.

Tactic 27: Rotating Acrostics

☑ Academic Discussion
☑ Active Participation
☑ Formative Processes and Tools

Students *construct* acrostics that *summarize* key points learned during an intentionally chunked presentation or text. This technique engages all learners as they move about the classroom discussing concepts, negotiating words, making connections, and composing concise statements or phrases to capture the gist of content.

How It Works

1. Identify a single term to use as the focal point for the lesson you are planning to present to your students. For example, if your lesson will introduce students to the three branches of government, you might select *balance* as a target term for the acrostics.

2. Divide your presentation into segments, taking into account the number of letters in the target term. Thus, if *balance* is your target term, you might divide your presentation on the branches of government into seven chunks. Each chunk should contain enough new information for students to consider, but not too much for them to process before another chunk is presented.

3. Divide your students into **NUMBERED HEADS** groups. Pre-plan these groups for social and academic compatibility to avoid behavior challenges as students move about the room.

4. Prepare a sheet of chart paper for each group by writing the letters of your target term vertically down the left margin. Post the sheets around the room. If space is limited, consider moving to the hall or a larger space for that day or post the chart paper for each group at the group's table.

5. Present the first chunk of information. For example, you might say, "When planning the design of the federal government, delegates at the Constitutional Convention were concerned that if any one person or group had too much power, the country would end up under the rule of a dictator or tyrant. So they decided to divide the powers of the federal government into three different branches."

6. Give groups a few minutes to deliberate and pinpoint the gist of the new information. They should then generate a succinct sentence or phrase that represents that gist. The requisite for the sentence or phrase is that it must begin with one of the letters in the target term. For example, one group might record "Can't let one group have too much power" for C. Another group might record "Avoiding rule under dictator or tyrant" for one of the A's.

7. Allow a few groups to share their thinking, using **NUMBERED HEADS** to designate the spokesperson, and perhaps a **RESPONSE FRAME** to promote scholarly discussion. This quick review and check for understanding gives you and students immediate feedback.

8. Before you present a new chunk of information, have students rotate to the next posted chart paper. If you are hesitant about moving the students, then have groups rotate their papers to the next group. Either way, students should read what the previous group wrote as they prepare to hear the next chunk of information and generate an addition to the acrostic before them.

9. Present the next segment. Remind students that they must generate a sentence or phrase for a letter not already used in the acrostic they currently have.

10. Continue the process until you have presented all information and all letters of the target word have been accounted for. As a class, vote for the finished acrostic that best represents the new information shared, thus presenting another opportunity for students to make sense of the new content.

Both Senate and House of Representatives make up Congress.

Avoid giving one group or person too much power.

Laws made by Congress.

Appointment to Supreme Court has to be approved by Senate.

New government divided into three branches.

Constitution interpreted by judicial branch.

Executive branch headed by President.

Tactic 28: Sift, Sort, and Summarize

☑ Thoughtful Work
☑ Meaningful Work
☑ Formative Processes and Tools

Students *sift* through content terms, *sort* the terms into student-generated categories, and use the categories to *summarize* content learned. Just as **PROBABLE PASSAGE** reveals understanding and misconceptions before learning, **SIFT, SORT, AND SUMMARIZE** conveys the extent to which students make sense of new instructional content and where instructional adjustments need to be made.

How It Works

- **Preparation.** Select 15–20 terms related to the recent unit of study. The terms can be names, places, symbols, equations, or even images. Before distributing the terms to students, create a document with each term in a separate box using a table format. Prepare a set for each **PARTNER A/PARTNER B** pair or **NUMBERED HEADS** group by cutting the terms into separate slips and placing one set each in a snack-size bag or envelope. Consider copying the terms on different colors of paper to avoid groups mixing up terms. Also give students several sticky notes for labeling their sorts. Here is an example of terms for students to use after a unit of study on plants.

seed	stamen	petal	pollen
fibrous root	veins	germinate	ripen
annual	style	pistil	perennial
photosynthesis	taproot	anther	node
xylem	chlorophyll	phloem	carbon dioxide

- **Sift**. Tell students to sift through the terms and filter out the ones that no one in the groups knows or understands. Ask students to put those terms to the side so as you walk around you can assess which terms need more clarification.
- **Sort**. Instruct students to now sort the terms into three, four, or five groups based on meaning. Students should use the sticky notes to label each sort group with a specific name. Allow each group to share the labels they use. When needed, ask for clarification, elaboration, and justification.
- **Summarize**. For individual assessment of learning, ask each student to summarize the content by writing a sentence or paragraph about one of the sorted groups, highlighting each term in that category.

Consider this modification of the technique to use with primary-age students.

- Print each word in bold lettering on individual sentence strips or large paper.
- Give each student a word. Ask each student to think about how his or her word connects to what was learned.
- Identify the categories for the words. Post the category labels in the front of the room or possibly in **FOUR CORNERS**.
- Students now do a "sort" as each student moves to the labeled space or corner that best represents the group for his or her word.

Tactic 29: Summarization Pyramid

☑ Academic Discussion
☑ Formative Processes and Tools

Students *summarize* new instructional content with short answers that represent key concepts and connections to those concepts. Rick Wormeli (2005) describes this tool as "wonderfully versatile" because of the variety of formats, sizes, and prompts teachers can design with it to provide closure of a learning segment.

How It Works

1. Give students a blank pyramid like the following example, or have students construct a pyramid of lines on paper, creating several blank boxes. You can also give students sticky notes to arrange on their desks or on paper in the shape of a pyramid. A pyramid of five or six lines is adequate, but you can have students create longer or shorter ones.

2. For the first line, present a prompt for students to fill a single word related to the unit of study in the top blank box of the pyramid. For example, you might ask for one word that sums up the information learned. That could be a key vocabulary term, a character's name, or the topic. Increase engagement and quickly check for understanding by briefly pausing and inviting students to share ideas.

3. Continue to the line with two blank boxes. Present a prompt that ask students for two words or two ideas, one for each blank box. For example, you could ask for two adjectives that describe the word in the first box. Again, briefly pause and ask students to share ideas.

4. Continue presenting prompts one line at a time, always pausing to hear student thinking. Other ideas for prompts include three actions related to the topic, four concrete examples, a five-word new title for the text or presentation, a six-word question that was or was not answered in the text or presentation.

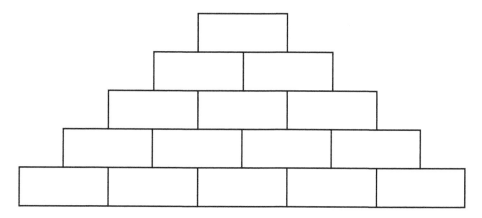

Tactic 30: Tableaux

☑ Meaningful Work
☑ Active Participation

Students *examine* content and *construct* frozen pictures or statues to represent what they understand about key topics within a unit of study. This technique promotes creative thinking skills as students collaborate in small groups to generate, associate, and hypothesize ideas to make sense of new information.

How It Works

- **Generate**. Each small group chooses or is assigned a topic (a vocabulary term, a process or sequence, a basic fact, an abstract concept, etc.) related to newly learned information. Working quietly so as to not reveal their topic, groups spend five to ten minutes examining their topic through a closer lens and generating a list of the characteristics or features that make it unique. For example, a second-grade group learning about text features might select *index* as their topic and list features such as *alphabetized, lists, page numbers, back of book,* and *points to.* Or a ninth-grade biology group studying biomes might choose *tundra* as their topic and list features such as *extremely cold, little precipitation, simple vegetation, short growth season,* and *dead organic material for nutrients.*

- **Associate**. Groups associate those characteristics or features with gestures, facial expressions, posture, and movement of the human body. They then combine all of their ideas to create one frozen statue or scene that uses every group member's body to represent the key attributes of their topic. Consider the second graders exploring the concept of the index of a book. One student sits on the floor with his arms shaped like the letter *C*. Behind him, a student sits in a chair and creates a lower case *B* with her arms. A third student stands behind her and creates the letter *A*. Their vertical pose represents the linear structure of an index, as a fourth student stands to the side and points to one letter.

- **Hypothesize.** Each group presents its tableau to the class. Peers interpret the frozen pictures to figure out what topic is being represented. The class assesses each tableau for clarity and accuracy by suggesting what attributes of the topic each group member represented. To extend discussion, students speculate how allowing movement within the tableau would impact the interpretation. For example, what would happen if the student pointing to one letter of the frozen index points to a different letter?

Tactic 31: Upside-Down Teaching

☑ Thoughtful Work
☑ Learning Environment
☑ Formative Processes and Tools

Students *analyze* a problem, and possibly with productive struggle, build new content process knowledge. Mathematics educator, speaker, and writer Cathy Seeley prefers this technique instead of the **GRADUAL RELEASE FRAMEWORK**, especially when it comes to teaching mathematical thinking (Seeley, 2014). She describes this tactic as a more student-centered approach that begins with a worthy problem and places students in a more active role in learning. In other words, rather than teachers modeling step-by-step procedural knowledge, students begin learning by testing their own thinking and approaches toward a solution.

How It Works

- Give students a task worthy of rigorous thinking. Refer to page 79 as you assess the task for the appropriate level of thinking and level of difficulty. Allow students to work with partners or small groups to tackle the task before you explicitly teach them related strategies or procedural knowledge to complete the task. Observe student conversations and processes to assess information gaps and adjust future instruction. Be mindful that this approach may require more time and effective classroom management, but yields increased student engagement and learning connections.

- Gather as a whole class to discuss the questions, struggles, clarifications, and aha moments students experienced while wrestling with the task. Use **NUMBERED HEADS** to designate a spokesperson for each group and **RESPONSE FRAMES** to encourage scholarly dialogue as students share the different ways they approached the task. Look for opportunities to acknowledge risk-taking and ownership of learning, as students self-reflect, set new learning goals, and possibly emerge with meaningful procedural knowledge.

- Use your observations from the small group and feedback from the whole class discussion to intentionally design instruction. Where do students need direct instruction and explicit examples? How do you need to adjust the instructional pace? Where would differentiated instruction be useful?

Tactic 32: Word Banks

☑ Academic Discussion
☑ Meaningful Work
☑ Learning Environment

Students *refine* thinking as they contribute and extract words from a student-generated or teacher-generated stockpile of related words. Temporary or permanently fixed, word banks are not spelling lists, vocabulary lists, or even lists of words to study for an upcoming quiz. Word Banks are student-friendly tools to amplify scholarly language and foster creativity. In fact, students are encouraged to take risks and incorporate both familiar and unfamiliar words when speaking and writing.

Student-Generated

Invite students to brainstorm words related to content or writing topics. Use **GIVE ONE/GET ONE** and **IDEA WAVES** to collect the words students contribute. Engage students by allowing them to record the words on chart paper or sentence strips and post in the classroom. Shape the brainstorming session by designating the types of words students should gather. For example, students can brainstorm topic-related words that are verbs, nouns, or adjectives. Or the class can work together to brainstorm 26 words from *A* to *Z* related to the topic. Keep the bank of words posted as students use the words to complete speaking and writing tasks. Some teachers ask students to underline the words they used in their writing.

Teacher-Generated

Create and distribute small portable word banks for students to use for a variety of tasks. For example, distribute banks of transitions that students can keep in notebooks and use when writing. Often teachers format these mini word banks as bookmarks or laminated strips for desks.

Transitions			
List of Ideas	**Sequential Order**	**Compare/ Contrast**	**Cause and Effect**
• To begin with • Besides • Several • For example • For instance • In addition • In fact • Most important • Equally important • To illustrate	• After a while • Before • Gradually • In the meantime • Initially • Later • Meanwhile • Not long after • Since • Soon	• Although • Conversely • Either/neither • Even though • However • Not only • On one hand • Otherwise • Rather than • Similarly	• As a result • As expected • Because of • Consequently • Due to • In effect • For this reason • Nevertheless • So that • Subsequently

Tactic 33: Word Wall Workout

☑ Academic Discussion
☑ Learning Environment
☑ Formative Processes and Tools

Students *analyze, synthesize,* and *evaluate* academic and domain-specific vocabulary to strengthen classroom reading, writing, and discussion. Words are gradually added to the wall and organized in a student-friendly system. Word walls to reinforce spelling and high-frequency sight words are often arranged alphabetically. However, teachers and students can post words to the wall based on a variety of classifications (parts of speech, unit of study, academic or content, etc.).

When setting up word walls, keep in mind that the words must be:

- bold enough and large enough for ALL students to see
- added on to gradually instead of all words posted at one time
- reinforced in everything students read, write, and discuss in class

In the following chart, there are 30 ways to "move" students to become familiar with the words on the wall. These tactics work well as entrance and exit tickets, extra credit on assessments, and fillers for transitions from one task to another.

Word Wall Workout		
Analyze	**Synthesize**	**Evaluate**
Break down the word with the most letters on the wall. Is it also the word with the most syllables? Explain.	*Blend* two words on the wall into one new word. What does the new word mean?	*Assess* the instruction of the words on the wall. Which word was explained the best? How?
Classify two words on the wall as elementary, two as middle-school, and two as high-school level words.	*Build* a one-minute dance sequence to explain one word on the wall.	*Award* one word on the wall "My Favorite Word on the Wall." Explain your choice.
Compare two words on the wall that begin with the same letter. How else are they alike?	*Compose* a question to ask a famous person (living or dead) using two words on the wall.	*Judge* the appearance of the words on the wall. Which word looks the most captivating? Suggest a reason for that.
Contrast the way one word on the wall in this classroom might be used differently in another classroom.	*Connect* one word on the wall in this classroom to a word on the wall in another subject. Explain the connection.	*Measure* your extended usage of the words on the wall. List one word you have used outside of this classroom. Explain.
Divide one word on the wall into the prefix and root word. Use what you know about the prefix or root to explain what the word means.	*Create* a simile or metaphor to compare one word on the wall with a specific food, color, sport, weekday, or number.	*Rank* ten words on the wall from "least to most likely to use in the real world."

Word Wall Workout (continued)		
Analyze	**Synthesize**	**Evaluate**
Examine two words on the wall that have opposite meanings. Identify one way they are alike.	*Design* an original symbol to represent one word on the wall.	*Rate* the usage of the words on the wall. Which word was used more today than any other word?
Inventory the words on the wall. Are there more nouns, verbs, or adjectives?	*Generate* one test question that incorporates three words on the wall.	*Select* one word on the wall to remove. Explain your reasoning.
Sift through the words on the wall to identify one word that can be a noun and a verb.	*Imagine* a class reunion for several words on the wall. Who would be invited and why?	*Recommend* one word to add to the wall. Defend your choice.
Sort nine words on the wall into three groups of three based on meaning. Label each group.	*Revise* a title of a current or past TV show using a word on the wall.	*Suggest* a way to remember how to pronounce the most challenging word on the wall to say.
Survey the words on the wall and predict three that will be used in the next unit of study.	*Summarize* a current news event using two words on the wall.	*Weigh* the value of the words on the wall. Which word should remain on the wall all year?

Appendix

References

Chapter One

Anderson, L. W. & Krathwohl, D. R., Eds. (2001). *A taxonomy for learning, teaching and assessing: A revision of Bloom's taxonomy of educational objectives*. Boston: Allyn & Bacon.

Bagley, M. (2013). *George Washington Carver: Biography, inventions & quotes*. Retrieved from http://www.livescience.com/41780-george-washington-carver.html.

Carver, G. W. (1922). Letter from Carver to Pammel, May 5, 1922. Retrieved from http://cdm15031.contentdm.oclc.org/cdm/fullbrowser/collection/p15031coll7/id/47/rv/compoundobject/cpd/52.

Merritt, R. H. (1929). *From captivity to fame or The life of George Washington Carver*, page 30. Boston: Meador. Retrieved from George Washington Carver: Advocate for southern farmers: highlights (2004). Documenting the American South. http://docsouth.unc.edu/highlights/carver.html.

Vella, C. (2015). *George Washington Carver: A life*. Baton Rouge, LA: Louisiana State University Press.

Chapter Two

Anderson, L. W. & Krathwohl, D. R., Eds. (2001). *A taxonomy for learning, teaching and assessing: A revision of Bloom's taxonomy of educational objectives.* Boston: Allyn & Bacon.

Kashdan, T. (2009). *Curious? Discover the missing ingredient to a fulfilling life.* New York: William Morrow.

Leslie, I. (October 12, 2014). "Google makes us all dumber: The neuroscience of search engines." *Salon.* Retrieved from http://www.salon.com/2014/10/12/google_makes_us_all_dumber_the_neuroscience_of_search_engines/.

Leslie, I. (2015). *Curious: The desire to know and why your future depends on it.* New York: Basic Books.

Pink, D. H. (2011). *Drive: The surprising truth about what motivates us.* New York: Riverhead Books.

University of Rochester Medical Center (n.d.). "Understanding the teen brain." Retrieved from https://www.urmc.rochester.edu/encyclopedia/content.aspx?ContentTypeID=1&ContentID=3051.

Chapter Three

Brown, J. R. & Fehige, Y. (2016). "Thought experiments." In E. N. Zalta, Ed., *The Stanford encyclopedia of philosophy.* Retrieved from http://plato.stanford.edu/entries/thought-experiment.

Duhigg, C. (2014). *The power of habit: why we do what we do in life and business.* New York: Random House.

Gregoire, C. (2013). "Research uncovers how and where imagination occurs in the brain." *Huffington Post.* Retrieved from http://www.huffingtonpost.com/2013/09/17/imagination-brain_n_3922136.html.

Jobs, S. (2005). Commencement address at Stanford University, Stanford, CA, June 12, 2005.

King, S. (2010). *On writing: 10th anniversary edition: A memoir of the craft.* New York: Scribner.

Chapter Four

Association for Psychological Science News (October 14, 2010). "Young children are especially trusting of things they're told." Retrieved from http://www.psychologicalscience.org/index.php/news/releases/young-children-are-especially-trusting-of-things-theyre-told.html.

Balls, A. (2013). "The flattening of corporate management." The NBER Digest. Retrieved from http://www.nber.org/digest/oct03/w9633.html.

Blakely, S. (n.d.). "Sara Blakely dared to ask, 'Why not?'" (video file). Retrieved from http://www.inc.com/sara-blakely/the-spanx-story-how-sara-blakely-turned-footless-pantyhose-into-a-business.html.

Davies, A., Fidler, D., & Gorbis. D. (2011). "Future work skills 2020." Palo Alto, CA: Institute for the Future for University of Phoenix Research Institute. Retrieved from http://www.iftf.org/uploads/media/SR1382A_UPRI_future_work_skills_sm.pdf.

Cherry, K. (April 20, 2016). "What is authoritarian parenting?" Retrieved from https://www.verywell.com/what-is-authoritarian-parenting-2794955.

Frank, R. (October 16, 2013). "Billionaire Sara Blakely says secret to success is failure." Retrieved from http://www.cnbc.com/2013/10/16/billionaire-sara-blakely-says-secret-to-success-is-failure.html.

Pink, D. H. (2011). *Drive: The surprising truth about what motivates us.* New York: Riverhead Books.

Tartakovsky, M. (April 4, 2014). "Helping your kids set boundaries." *World of Psychology*. Retrieved from http://psychcentral.com/blog/ archives/2014/04/11/helping-your-kids-set-boundaries/.

University of New Hampshire (February 10, 2012). "Controlling parents more likely to have delinquent children." *Science Daily*. Retrieved from www.sciencedaily.com/releases/2012/02/120210105901.htm.

Wirthman, L. (August 19, 2013). "Sara Blakely first woman billionaire to sign giving pledge." Retrieved from http://www.forbes.com/ sites/northwesternmutual/2013/08/19/sara-blakely-first-woman-billionaire-giving-it-away/#536ac4521237.

Chapter Five

Brookhart, S. (2014). *How to design questions and tasks to assess student thinking*. Alexandria, VA: Association for Supervision & Curriculum Development.

Caldwell, J. & Ford, M. (2002). *Where have all the bluebirds gone? How to soar with flexible grouping*. Portsmouth, NH: Heinemann.

Cazden, C. (1988). *Classroom discourse: The language of teaching and learning*. Portsmouth, NH: Heinemann.

Gallagher, Kelly (2004). *Deeper reading: Comprehending challenging texts, 4-12*, page 106. Portland, ME: Stenhouse.

Marzano, R. J. (2013). "Art and science of teaching/asking questions—at four different levels." *Educational Leadership: Creativity Now!* 70(5), 76-77. Retrieved from http://www.ascd.org/publications/educational-leadership/feb13/vol70/num05/Asking-Questions%E2%80%94At-Four-Different-Levels.aspx.

Zwiers, J. & Crawford, M. (2011). *Academic conversations: Classroom talk that fosters critical thinking and content understandings*. Portland, ME: Stenhouse.

Chapter Six

Bellanca, J. A., Fogarty, R., & Pete, B. M. (2012). *How to teach thinking skills within the common core: 7 key student proficiencies of the new national standards.* Bloomington, IN: Solution Tree.

Brookhart, S. (2014). *How to design questions and tasks to assess student thinking.* Alexandria, VA: Association for Supervision & Curriculum Development.

Clark, R., Ed. (2001). *Learning from media: Arguments, analysis and evidence,* page 2. Charlotte, NC: Information Age Publishing.

Coleman, D. (2011). "Bringing the Common Core to life," Part 4. Albany, NY: New York State Education Department. Retrieved from http://usny.nysed.gov/rttt/docs/bringingthecommoncoretolife/part4transcript.pdf.

Drapeau, P. (2014). *Sparking student creativity: Practical ways to promote innovative thinking and problem solving,* Chapter 1. Alexandria, VA: Association for Supervision & Curriculum Development.

McTighe, J. & Wiggins, G. P. (2013). *Essential questions: Opening doors to student understanding,* page 3. Alexandria, VA: Association for Supervision & Curriculum Development.

Learning Network (2016). "What's going on in this picture?" *New York Times.* Retrieved from http://learning.blogs.nytimes.com/category/lesson-plans/whats-going-on-in-this-picture/.

Sheninger, E. (February 18, 2016). "5 ways digital tools are transforming the education space." *EdTech Magazine.* Retrieved from http://www.edtechmagazine.com/k12/article/2016/02/5-ways-digital-tools-are-transforming-education-space.

Wormeli, R. (2009). *Metaphors and analogies: Power tools for teaching any subject.* Portland, ME: Stenhouse.

Chapter Seven

Duckworth, A (2016). *Grit: The power of passion and perseverance.* New York: Scribner. Retrieved from http://angeladuckworth.com/qa/.

Jackson, R. R. (2009). *Never work harder than your students & other principles of great teaching,* page 173. Alexandria, VA: Association for Supervision and Curriculum Development.

Jensen, E. (2005). *Teaching with the brain in mind,* page 35. Alexandria, VA: Association for Supervision and Curriculum Development.

Sousa, D. (2011). *How the brain learns,* page 70. Thousand Oaks, CA: Corwin.

Tomlinson, C. A. & McTighe, J. (2006). *Integrating differentiated instruction and understanding by design: Connecting content and kids.* Alexandria, VA: Association for Supervision and Curriculum Development.

Chapter Eight

Frey, N. & Fisher, D. (2011). "Chapter 1: Creating a Formative Assessment System" in *The formative assessment action plan: Practical steps to more successful teaching and learning.* Alexandria, VA: Association for Supervision and Curriculum Development.

Raphael, T., Highfield, K., & Au, K. (2006). *QAR now: A powerful and practical framework that develops comprehension and higher-level thinking in all students,* page 27. New York: Scholastic.

Rothstein, D. & Santana, L. (2011). *Make just one change: Teach students to ask their own questions.* Boston: Harvard Education Press.

Seeley, C. (2014). *Smarter than we think.* New York: Scholastic.

Wormeli, R. (2005). *Summarization in any subject: 50 Techniqes to improve student learning,* page 155. Alexandria, VA: Association for Supervision and Curriculum Development.